EAT WELL

BE WELL

EAT WELL

Plant-Based · Gluten-Free · Refined Sugar-Free

BE WELL

100+ Healthy Re-creations of the Food You Crave

JANA CRISTOFANO

STERLING EPICURE

New York

STERLING EPICURE
New York

An Imprint of Sterling Publishing Co., Inc.
1166 Avenue of the Americas
New York, NY 10036

ISBN 978-1-4549-3377-9

Library of Congress Cataloging-in-Publication Data

Names: Cristofano, Jana, author.
Title: Eat well, be well : 100+ healthy re-creations of the food you crave / Jana Cristofano.
Description: New York : Sterling Publishing Co., Inc., [2020] | Includes index. | Summary: "Satisfy your cravings
  and boost your vitality with good food that tastes great and is vegan"-- Provided by publisher.
Identifiers: LCCN 2019019084 | ISBN 9781454933779 | ISBN 9781454933991 (epub)
Subjects: LCSH: Cooking (Natural foods) | Gluten-free diet--Recipes. | Sugar-free diet--Recipes. | Vegan cooking.
Classification: LCC TX741 .C75 2020 | DDC 641.5/6362--dc23
LC record available at https://lccn.loc.gov/2019019084

Distributed in Canada by Sterling Publishing Co., Inc.
c/o Canadian Manda Group, 664 Annette Street
Toronto, Ontario M6S 2C8, Canada
Distributed in the United Kingdom by GMC Distribution Services
Castle Place, 166 High Street, Lewes, East Sussex BN7 1XU, England
Distributed in Australia by NewSouth Books
University of New South Wales, Sydney, NSW 2052, Australia

For information about custom editions, special sales, and premium and corporate purchases, please contact
Sterling Special Sales at 800-805-5489 or specialsales@sterlingpublishing.com.

Manufactured in Singapore

2 4 6 8 10 9 7 5 3 1

sterlingpublishing.com

Cover design by David Ter-Avanesyan
Interior design by Shannon Nicole Plunkett

Additional interior photography credits: Christopher Bain (© Sterling Publishing Co., Inc.):
ii-iii, vi, 22, 48, 74, 96, 122, 142, 170, 212
Cover credits: Main photograph © Ina Peters/Stocksy United; Food inside the dish by Elena_Danileiko/iStock;
Back cover author photo by David Cristofano

Contents

Introduction
and
Guiding Principles

*Y*ou want it all.

You want to eat food that is mouth-watering, get-in-your-belly delicious and not suffer any adverse health effects. Why stop there? You want to enjoy food that is crave-worthy while promoting health and healing in your body.

Impossible, you say? Healthy food is boring and unexciting? Maintaining a nutritious diet is impossible? I used to think so too. But what do you do when you realize that comfort food is no longer comforting? Or becomes downright discomforting: diabetes, cardiac disease, obesity, arthritis, migraines—the list goes on. Study after study suggests that what we put on our plate is making all the difference.

But diet can be both the cure and the cause.

Over the years I repeatedly sought change, knowing a nutritious diet offered the promise of a healthier and happier life. I would press fresh juices, eat salads, and snack on nuts.

And as you might guess, my energy level would increase and the number on the scale would decrease. I had a little skip in my step! But regardless of the results, I'd return to my old ways of eating.

As the saying goes, necessity proved to be the mother of invention. Years passed and my health issues began to accumulate: struggles with infertility and miscarriage, battles with migraine headaches and arthritis, blood sugar levels that put me on the path toward diabetes—a path widened by my family history. And physically, I noticed the on-and-off pounds were mostly on or accumulating.

So I set upon a quest for knowledge. What was once a pastime became a passion. My consumption of health and diet books kicked into overdrive. I took classes that were based on a variety of nutritional models. I compared and contrasted every diet and nutritional approach I could find. The union of these concepts became obvious. A spectrum of health issues can be improved or corrected by eliminating four dietary categories: animal products, gluten, refined sugars, and unhealthy fats. Each one is an agent of inflammation and disease.

So what's left? What *can* I eat?

The answer is to eat a plant-based, gluten-free, and refined sugar–free diet and empower your body to *heal itself*. You don't have to look far to find data that support the impact of diet and nutrition as it positively correlates to health, but Hippocrates said it best, "Let food be thy medicine, and medicine be thy food." But for me to succeed in eating as suggested by my research, I knew I needed those to-die-for recipes that would satisfy not just my body, but my palate and my mind. I needed to *crave* this food.

And so my mission began. My approach to eating better became one of deconstruction and reconstruction. I couldn't bear the thought of no longer eating my favorite foods, yet my quality of life depended on it. I systematically broke down traditional dishes by ingredient, type, and purpose. After identifying healthier, gluten-free, plant-based, and refined sugar–free ingredients, I created original dishes and customized classic favorites. Success was measured first by my own palate, then the palates of others. I wanted to know, "Did it taste good? Was it so incredible that I could imagine never eating the traditional version again?" The answers were repeatedly yes.

So what about my health?

After eating this way, my blood sugar levels returned to the normal range. The migraines disappeared. Aches from arthritis, gone. As I started to feel better, look healthier, and naturally lose extra pounds, conversations about diet occurred with greater frequency. Coworkers, friends, and family would ask, "How did you do it? You look great. You have so much energy!" By answering that I was eliminating gluten, animal products, and refined sugars and replacing them with plant-based foods, I would be faced with glazed-over eyes. "Oh, you're eating bird food. I could never do that."

But you *can* eat nutritious dishes and still have a gastronomical experience. I wanted to inspire others to achieve the same sense of health and wellness while enjoying all of the fabulous flavors and textures this culinary lifestyle has to offer. That foodie inside of you will be happier than ever, and healthier too!

While sharing my recipes through my blog, *Nutritionicity*, I have had the honor and privilege of getting to know so many fabulous people: You might be someone who wants to improve your overall health through a plant-based diet or address a specific health issue that a medical professional has advised you to do through diet; perhaps you suffer from food allergies and the accompanying symptoms; you might be someone who cares passionately for the environment and wants to act in kindness to all creatures; or you might seek delicious cuisine that tantalizes your taste buds and makes your mind and body feel harmoniously pleased. Whoever you are, you are welcome here. *You* have warmed my heart and inspired *me* with your stories. Many of you have attributed part of your success at becoming healthier and maintaining diet-related changes to the ability to enjoy delicious dishes you thought you'd never be able to eat again.

So many of you have encouraged me to create this book, and I am forever grateful. I assembled this compilation of recipes to include some of the most popular recipes from the blog, some with enhancements, and a majority of new recipes, many of which are my all-time favorites. My hope is for this recipe collection to meet you wherever you are in your unique journey to health and wellness.

Each of the 100+ recipes in this cookbook is gluten-free, plant-based/vegan, and refined sugar–free. A number of selections are either oil-free and/or nut-free or provide options for substitutions. Whether you are suffering from celiac disease, gluten sensitivity, or dairy allergies, are looking to take steps toward general well-being, hope to achieve weight loss, or want to consume a kinder and more environmentally friendly diet, this collection is for *you*. These dishes are designed to meet individual needs while sacrificing neither taste nor the culinary experience in the process.

I titled this collection *Eat Well, Be Well,* as my goal is not to place a mandate before you but an instrument of change. I am passionate about encouraging you with a *better-than-yesterday* approach. Failure doesn't need to be a part of the equation. Let's focus on progress, not perfection. Ask yourself these two simple questions. When I look back, do I see that I am moving forward? Am I better today than I was yesterday? Focusing on progress instead of perfection makes healthier living a real and sustainable aspect of life.

Enjoy! Eat well and be well soon!

Guiding Principles

With so many different terms used today and so many interpretations to describe the style of food or diet represented in this book, I wanted to clarify the terminology I use and its context.

WHAT IS WHOLE FOOD PLANT-BASED?
Whole food plant-based eating means consuming no animal products or by-products (i.e., meat, fish, dairy, eggs, honey). It consists of unrefined and unprocessed whole fruit, vegetables, grains, beans, legumes, nuts, and seeds.

WHAT IS PLANT-BASED?

A plant-based diet consists of the same ingredients as a whole food plant-based diet with occasional conservative use of some minimally processed ingredients. These include flours made from ground whole grains, natural sweeteners that still contain nutrients resulting in a lower glycemic index, and healthier oils. For examples, see Chapter 1, The Plant-Based, Gluten-Free Kitchen (page 11).

WHAT IS A VEGAN DIET?

Like the whole food plant-based and the plant-based diets, a vegan diet consists of no animal-based products or by-products. The vegan diet can include processed and refined foods, including white flour, refined sugar, and oil.

WHAT IS GLUTEN-FREE?

A gluten-free food does not contain any ingredients that have gluten proteins in them. Gluten proteins are found most commonly in grains like wheat, barley, and rye; however, this is not an exhaustive list. Oats are inherently gluten-free, but it should be noted that cross contamination can occur where they are grown, as well as during factory processing. It is best to buy oats or oat flour that has been certified gluten-free.

WHAT IS REFINED SUGAR–FREE?

The recipes in this book are refined sugar–free. This does *not* mean that they are sugar-free. It does mean that whatever sweetener is used in a recipe (i.e., maple syrup, coconut sugar, coconut nectar) has not undergone any chemical processing. In fact, most employ only minimal processing, thereby retaining some of the nutrients and keeping them closer to their natural state.

WHY EAT PLANT-BASED?

Many studies have been conducted and have drawn a cause-and-effect relationship between diet (as a permanent way of eating) and health. Probably the most notable study of nutrition was conducted by Dr. T. Colin Campbell, Professor Emeritus of Nutritional Biochemistry at Cornell University, in conjunction with Oxford University and the Chinese Academy of Preventative Medicine, known as the China Project. A longitudinal study that lasted twenty years, it was able to draw a host of statistically significant correlations between lifestyle, diet, and disease. The research strongly connected a plant-based diet to a lower risk of cancer, heart disease, and autoimmune disorders. If you are interested in a deep dive into the science and scientific data behind these conclusions, Dr. Campbell and his son Thomas M. Campbell II, MD outlined it in their book *The China Study*.

But it's not just about the data. The proof of the pudding is in the plant-based eating! Every day, more doctors are prescribing diet modifications instead of prescription drugs to treat—and in some cases reverse—disease. Dr. Caldwell Esselstyn, Jr., a former president of the staff of the renowned Cleveland Clinic, fellow of the American College of Cardiology, and surgeon did just that. Many years ago, Dr. Esselstyn experienced groundbreaking results when he treated cardiac patients with a whole food, plant-based, oil-free diet. After just a few *months* on a plant-based eating plan, patients began to experience significant improvement. Twenty years later, many patients who had been given one year to live remain symptom-free. For more details on Dr. Esselstyn's treatment success with a plant-based diet, read his book *Prevent and Reverse Heart Disease.*

Dr. Neal Barnard, founder of the Physician's Committee for Responsible Medicine, fellow of the American College of Cardiology, clinical researcher, and adjunct associate professor of medicine at the George Washington University School of Medicine and Health Sciences, uses a whole food, plant-based diet to treat and reverse the symptoms of type 2 diabetes. His book *Dr. Neal Barnard's Program for Reversing Diabetes: The Scientifically Proven System for Reversing Diabetes Without Drugs* outlines his protocol and success stories. And if you need a little more inspiration to give up cheese, check out Dr. Barnard's book *The Cheese Trap.* Dr. Barnard sheds light on the potential dangers of cheese consumption like weight gain, high blood pressure, and arthritis.

He also explains how cheese becomes addictive, as it contains mild opiates that trigger the same brain receptors as heroin and morphine. You will never want cheese again. And that is coming from me, a recovering cheese addict.

WHY EAT GLUTEN-FREE?

According to the Celiac Disease Foundation, about one in every hundred people has celiac disease—*millions*—and the number is growing. Celiac disease is an autoimmune response to the gluten protein that damages the lining of the small intestine and compromises nutrient absorption. Simply put, it wreaks havoc on you and your digestive system. For some people, it puts them out of commission for days.

A related but slightly different issue for some folks is gluten sensitivity. Those with gluten sensitivity have not been diagnosed with celiac disease but experience many of the same symptoms. From digestive issues (i.e., gas/bloating, abdominal cramping, diarrhea) to migraine headaches or arthritis-like pain to fatigue and even depression, gluten sensitivity can impact lives greatly.

And then there is wheat allergy, which is an allergic reaction to foods containing wheat. People with this particular issue can usually eat other gluten-containing foods, but not those derived specifically from wheat. Typical symptoms include hives/rashes, headaches, asthma, and even anaphylaxis.

In his book *Wheat Belly*, William Davis, MD, discusses *modern* wheat. Our wheat today has been genetically altered, like many genetically modified organisms, "to provide processed-food manufacturers the greatest yield at the lowest cost." Unfortunately, no research was done to ensure that these new versions of wheat would still be healthy for animals or humans to consume. Dr. Davis cites research by agricultural geneticists that demonstrates, "while 95 percent of the proteins expressed in the new (wheat) off-spring are the same, five percent are unique and found in neither parent." Some of these new unique proteins were identified as those associated with celiac disease.

Even if you are not suffering from any of the symptoms associated with gluten, it is likely that you know someone who is. With so many nutrient-rich and flavorful gluten-free flours today, you can make gluten discomfort a thing of the past—and make dishes that everyone you know can enjoy!

WHY EAT REFINED SUGAR–FREE?

Refined sugars are devoid of any nutrients and therefore absorbed into the bloodstream very quickly, resulting in a spike of insulin. Yes, unrefined sugars are still sugar and should be consumed in moderation. However, they are a healthier alternative to refined sugar sources. Since unrefined sugars retain some of their nutrients, they are not absorbed as quickly into the bloodstream and have a lower glycemic index (a measure of how slowly or quickly foods cause an increase in blood sugar).

SO YOU'VE NEVER EATEN PLANT-BASED OR GLUTEN-FREE? DON'T WORRY, THIS WON'T HURT A BIT.

As always, be sure to consult your health care provider before embarking on a new diet. If you're ready to begin, don't feel like you have to make an overnight leap. Some people have a lot of success with the cold turkey approach, but I have found that more often than not, slow and steady wins the race. Have you ever tried to wean yourself off caffeine? (Crazy, I know!) My diet is mostly clean. But sometimes I like to give my body a chance to do a little house cleaning by eliminating all caffeine, alcohol, and ingredients that are not a whole food. Before I do this, I slowly reduce my caffeine consumption over the course of the week prior. Rather than reduce my coffee consumption, I replace the caffeinated coffee with decaffeinated coffee a little more each day—removing the offender and replacing it with a better alternative.

When you are trying to remove other toxins from your diet, simply use the same method. The dairy products, processed sugar, and gluten all come with some withdrawal symptoms (headaches, colds, lethargy). Your body is cleaning out the gunk. But when you slowly remove these things by gradually increasing the healthier alternatives, your experience will be proportionately gentler.

The gradual approach also gives you a chance to adjust from a practical standpoint. Start by making some of the recipes in this cookbook that look and sound very appealing to you. Once you have a greater level of confidence in your ability to cook with a new style and enjoy the deliciousness of these recipes, you will feel empowered. As you add in more healthy foods, the unhealthy foods will become a thing of the past all on their own.

WHAT IF I SLIP?

It's all about balance and progress, not failure. Don't beat yourself up because you gave in to that craving for cheese, refined sugar, or gluten. Most of us have been there and done that. Dr. Neil Barnard makes a compelling argument in his book *The Cheese Trap* that cheese has an addictive component comparable to that of morphine. Most folks don't just like cheese; they're *hooked*. The good news is the longer you eat a cleaner diet the easier it gets. Your body will get its signals straightened out. As this happens, it will recognize the junk as junk; when you serve it up, you won't be happy. You may experience

digestive issues or congestion from the cheese or a migraine from the refined sugar. I know it sounds hard to believe now, but you will actually start to *crave* the healthier food.

BEFORE YOU START COOKING . . .

All of the recipes in this cookbook are plant-based, gluten-free, and refined sugar–free. They represent the spectrum within these parameters. Some are exceptionally nutritious, while others are superior alternatives to their unhealthy traditional counterparts. You can rest assured, your body and mind will be getting the most of what you make.

READ THE WHOLE RECIPE BEFORE YOU BEGIN.

This may seem obvious, but if you are new(er) to cooking plant-based and/or gluten-free, there are some significant paradigm shifts from the traditional recipes you're used to preparing or that were handed down for generations. For example, a recipe that uses flaxseed meal as a replacement for egg will require mixing the flaxseed meal with water (unless otherwise stated) and setting it aside for a few minutes to form a gelatinous mixture—in contrast to grabbing an egg and cracking it into a bowl in most traditional recipes. Be sure to review the entire recipe, from ingredients to method, before beginning so you can be best prepared.

ON INGREDIENTS

When I develop recipes, my goal is to make them not only healthier than most traditional dishes, but equally tasty. Many of the whole food plant-based recipes in this book also have no added sugar/sweetener or are oil-free. Some recipes contain small amounts of oil and added unrefined sugar sweeteners, such as coconut sugar, maple syrup, or coconut nectar. Diet is about balance. We all like to indulge in a treat once in a while. The key is making that indulgence as healthy as possible and eating it in moderation.

ON SUBSTITUTIONS

My recommendation is to make the recipe first as it is written, then tweak to your particular palate if you like. Here's why:

I have developed these recipes to serve as a starting point. Some people like more salt, garlic, or seasoning. Some like their baked goods crispy and not soft. Often I will suggest tasting a dish as you are making it to determine if you would prefer more seasoning. Just remember, you can always add more seasoning but you can't take it out. I frequently make suggestions for substitutions of ingredients. They are by no means comprehensive.

If you have an idea for a substitution, please keep a few things in mind. I crafted these recipes to have a specific taste and texture. Keeping them plant-based and gluten-free sometimes requires using certain ingredients for a purpose that is twofold—or different from what you might expect. For example, applesauce can double as a sweetener and a substitute for oil, but in some recipes it may be doing *both*, and removing it will impact the outcome. Additionally, certain starches (i.e., tapioca starch) are added to baked goods to add the chewy texture that gluten usually provides. If these starches are substituted with an alternative flour (i.e., almond meal) you may lose the desirable texture.

Dietary Features

Each recipe will have codes displayed, indicating the dietary features of the dish.

NAS – No added sugar

OF – Oil-free

OFO – Oil-free option

NF – Nut-free

NFO – Nut-free option

SF – Soy-free

PREP TIME AND COOK TIME

Each recipe features an active preparation time and cooking time, respectively. When a recipe features nuts that require soaking prior to beginning a recipe, the soak time will not be included in the active prep time, so please plan accordingly. That being said, soaking nuts and other advanced prep options *will* be mentioned in the Notes section. Additionally, recipes that have parallel cooking (for example, if squash is roasting in the oven while lentils cook on the stovetop) the time is counted concurrently.

NOTES

As previously stated, the Notes section will alert you if advance prep (i.e., soaking nuts) is required. Also included are helpful hints, substitutions, additional serving options, and options for advance prep.

Health and Nutrition Notes

Nutritional and health benefits will sometimes be provided to highlight exceptional aspects of certain ingredients, like these superstars, which are frequently used in the recipes:

Asparagus is ranked in the top twenty foods on the Aggregate Nutrition Density Index (ANDI). While boasting high levels of folate and vitamin K, it helps fight depression by preventing homocysteine levels from rising and interfering with dopamine, serotonin, and norepinephrine These are the neurotransmitters associated with mood or the happy chemicals in your brain.

Broccoli is loaded with vitamin C (one cup provides 135 percent of your daily value). It is a great source of vitamins A, B6, E, and K, fiber, calcium, magnesium, iron, zinc, niacin, and selenium. Broccoli also provides plant-based protein and some omega-3 fatty acids for good measure.

Buckwheat is not a grain, contrary to what its name implies. It is known as a pseudo-grain, similar to quinoa, and is the seed of a plant related to rhubarb. Loaded with all nine essential amino acids, buckwheat serves up a nice dose of a perfect and complete protein (see more on page 12). Buckwheat is a great source of B vitamins, manganese, magnesium, copper, calcium, and iron. It is also high in resistant fiber that helps lower blood sugar after meals, aiding in weight loss.

Cashews offer five grams of plant-based protein per one-ounce serving. They are nutrient rich with iron, vitamin B6, magnesium, copper, and phosphorus. Cashews are also beneficial for bone and skin health and help stabilize blood sugar.

Cauliflower is low in calories, fat, and carbs, while generous in fiber. It also offers 4 percent of your daily value of protein in one cup.

Plus, it offers 85 percent of your daily value of vitamin C in one cup. Cauliflower is also a great source of vitamin B6, vitamin K, magnesium, and potassium.

Chickpeas are a great source of plant-based protein and fiber, which has a favorable impact on blood sugar and overall colon health. They are also rich in iron, phosphate, calcium, magnesium, manganese, zinc, and vitamin K. Chickpeas also contain selenium, which is not present in a lot of fruits and vegetables. Selenium can act as an anti-inflammatory and aid in liver enzyme function. Current research, including what is found in the US National Library of Medicine National Institutes of Health, suggests that "chickpeas may help improve the nutrient profiles of meals."

Lentils are a great source of plant-based protein. They also offer a plentiful amount of soluble fiber, helping slow the metabolism of glucose from carbohydrates. By doing so, lentils are believed to have a very low impact on blood sugar compared to other grains and carbohydrates. They are also high in phosphorus, folate, magnesium, and iron.

Pineapple offers so much in the vitamin and mineral department. Just one cup serves more than 130 percent of your daily value of vitamin C, along with significant amounts of vitamin B6, magnesium, calcium, iron, and fiber.

Potato boasts healthy doses of potassium, magnesium, iron, calcium, and fiber. Plus, one medium potato contains 70 percent of your daily value of vitamin C, and 30 percent of vitamin B6. Potatoes are a great source of plant-based protein at four grams.

Quinoa is a great source of a complete plant-based protein. Quinoa is a very good source of magnesium, calcium, iron, phosphorous, B vitamins, and vitamin E. It is lower in carbohydrates than many grains because it is a pseudo-grain or seed. Plus, it has a low glycemic index because its carbohydrates are slow-releasing. This means the glucose is released more slowly and more steadily, helping maintain blood sugar levels.

CHAPTER 1

The Plant-Based, Gluten-Free Kitchen

I used to find cooking a means to an end. Now it's a means to multiple ends: health and happiness, community, and enjoyment. I love creating lip-smacking and palate-pleasing plant-based and gluten-free recipes. These recipes not only feed, nourish, and heal the body but also provide a sense of pleasure—to be enjoyed with others, even those (especially those!) who do not share the same diet you do.

You may share my sentiment about spending time cooking or you may prefer to simply sit down to a wonderfully prepared meal. Either way, it's likely we can all agree that simplifying the process is helpful. If you are fairly new to plant-based and/or gluten-free cooking, some of the ingredients may be different from those you usually stock in your pantry. This can feel intimidating or even daunting. I felt this way when I began experimenting with this style of food. But like any new style—fashion, dance, music, food—once you have a level of familiarity, you will embrace it and love it!

In this section I include highlights of the main ingredients I use frequently and helpful hints for cooking with them. Once you begin using these ingredients frequently, you will soon discover the joy of making your dishes so much healthier, tastier, and more satisfying. Plus, when cooking plant-based, gluten-free, and refined sugar–free, you will enjoy meals that satisfy your cravings and nourish your body.

Flours and Starches

There are so many gluten-free options available in flours and starches. Some offer more protein, vitamins, and minerals, and others have a flavor profile that can add a new dimension to a dish. There are even gluten-free flours that are great for creating baked goods that are as good as their gluten-containing counterparts—chewy and delicious!

TECHNIQUE FOR MEASURING GLUTEN-FREE FLOUR

Some flours are finer than others and will compress more when measured. For the sake of consistency I measure all flours and starches the same way: I hold the measuring cup in one hand and use a spoon to scoop the flour or starch into the measuring cup with the other. I fill until I have a *rounded cup* and *then very gently tap the flour or starch with the spoon while moving across the top of the measuring cup to remove the excess, resulting in a level cup of flour or starch.*

WATCH THE EXPIRATION DATES

Grains, nuts, and seeds contain oils. After a period of time these oils will start to break down and taint the flavor of your ingredient and, ultimately, the dish you are preparing. It is very important not to use expired ingredients. Some of these ingredients are expensive, so to prolong the life of grains, nuts, and seeds I store mine in sealed glass jars in the refrigerator. I write the name of the ingredient and the purchase date on an adhesive label and place it on the jar. These items should stay fresh up to six months, as a rule of thumb. If you can't spare the extra space in the fridge, try to store them in a cool, dark place.

GLUTEN-FREE FLOURS AND STARCHES

These ingredients are used throughout the book:

- **Almond meal or flour**—These are generally considered to be the same— finely ground nuts.
- **Arrowroot starch**
- **Brown rice flour**
- **Coconut flour**
- **Garbanzo or chickpea flour**
- **Gluten-free oat flour**—Make sure it is certified gluten-free. Although oats are inherently gluten-free, cross-contamination is possible.
- **Potato starch**—Unlike potato flour, which is made from cooked, dried, and ground potatoes, potato starch is solely the starch extracted from potatoes.
- **Sorghum flour**
- **Tapioca flour or starch**—Tapioca flour and tapioca starch are the same.
- **White rice flour**

Seeds, Nuts, Grains, Pseudo-Grains, and Legumes
(Get your protein here!)

One of the most common concerns people have about eating a plant-based diet is *how to get enough protein.* Well, you've come to the right place. Plant-based cuisine provides an abundance of protein through sources that your body can assimilate more easily.

If you are interested in the science behind it, allow me to expound. A complete protein is made up of twenty amino acids. The amino acid profile is not the same in every food. Many foods do not contain all twenty amino acids.

Nine of the twenty amino acids are called **essential amino acids**. This means that they are necessary to form a complete protein. Essential amino acids cannot be manufactured by the body, so you must get them from the food you consume. When we eat, our bodies store the amino acids from our food and then mix and match from varying food sources to build new complete proteins.

Some foods do contain all twenty amino acids and provide a complete protein. Meat, for example, is a **complete protein** but so are **quinoa, buckwheat, pumpkin seeds, and hemp seeds. Complementary proteins** are foods that work together to form a complete protein. Each provides the essential amino acids that the other is lacking. This is why it is important to eat a balanced diet with a variety of protein sources. For example, legumes and grains are complementary proteins. When you combine black beans and rice or black beans and corn, they provide an adequate amount of all of the essential amino acids and become a complete protein. Many fruits and vegetables contain protein as well, but these **seeds, nuts, grains, pseudo-grains, and legumes** are your heavy hitters.

Whenever possible I purchase raw or sprouted nuts and seeds. They are more flexible for cooking and in most cases easier to digest.

SEEDS, NUTS, GRAINS, PSEUDO-GRAINS, AND LEGUMES

Keep these ingredients on-hand in the pantry, as they are frequently used or suggested as substitutions throughout the book:

- **Almonds**
- **Black beans**
- **Black-eyed peas**
- **Buckwheat**
- **Cannellini beans**
- **Cashews**—A frequent replacement for a dairy ingredient in traditional recipes. cashews have a mild flavor and produce a smooth and creamy texture. Often I note when other nuts or seeds can be substituted.
- **Chia seeds**
- **Chickpeas or garbanzos**
- **Gluten-free oats**
- **Golden flaxseed meal**—Combined with water or plant-based milk, it forms a gel that can replace eggs. I prefer golden flaxseed meal over brown; it has a milder flavor and combines well with other ingredients.
- **Great Northern beans**
- **Lentils**
- **Macadamias**
- **Pecans**
- **Quinoa**
- **Red kidney beans**
- **Rice**
- **Shelled sunflower seeds**
- **Sprouted shelled pumpkin seeds or pepitas**
- **Walnuts**

Frequently Used Unrefined Sugars and Sweeteners

- **Brown Rice Syrup**—This syrup is made by adding enzymes to cooked whole grain rice to break down the starch into sugars.
- **Coconut nectar**—This thick syrup is the sap that comes from the flower on the coconut tree. It is evaporated at very low temperatures to allow it to thicken without compromising nutrients by exposing them to high heat.
- **Coconut sugar**—This sugar is made from the crystallization of the nectar of the coconut flower on the coconut tree. You may be surprised to find out that it does not taste like coconut. It is a brown sugar very similar in taste and texture to traditional brown sugar.
- **Date sugar**—This sugar is made from dehydrated dates that are ground to resemble granulated sugar. A small amount of fiber will remain undissolved in baked goods or hot liquids because the whole pitted fruit is used.
- **Frozen bananas**—When ripe bananas are frozen, the sugars in them become concentrated. Mashed frozen bananas make an excellent sweetener in dishes where banana flavor is a welcome addition. Check out how to freeze bananas (see page 18).
- **Maple sugar**—This sugar is made from the crystallization of the sap of the maple tree.
- **Maple syrup**—Maple syrup is made from the sap of the maple tree. When purchasing maple syrup, it should be pure. There should only be one ingredient on the ingredient list, pure maple syrup.
- **Medjool dates**—Grinding pitted dates into a paste makes a great sweetener for many dishes.

Oils, Fats, and Substitutes

OILS

When cooking, I try to use oils that remain stable at higher temperatures, like avocado or walnut. Olive oil and grapeseed oil are nice for medium temperature cooking or salad dressings. Coconut oil is perfect for when structure is required, such as a frosting or "cheesecake," as it is solid at room temperature. I use refined coconut oil when I don't want any added coconut flavor, and virgin coconut oil when coconut flavor might enhance the dish.

- **Avocado oil**
- **Coconut oil**
- **Grapeseed oil**
- **Olive oil**
- **Walnut oil**

OIL SUBSTITUTES

In some cases a recipe may need fat, but it does not have to be oil. In these situations, nut and seed butters are perfect alternatives as they are healthier, whole food fats that provide rich creaminess without the use of oil. These are some of my favorite options.

- Almond butter
- Avocado
- Cashew butter
- Cashew cream
- Peanut butter
- Sunflower seed butter
- Tahini

FAT SUBSTITUTES

As with added sugars, I try to limit the use of oils, and sometimes fats in general, to situations where I feel a substitute would compromise the outcome of the dish. In these scenarios healthier ingredients can be used to replace oil in a recipe. These include:

- Bananas
- Unsweetened Applesauce

Plant-Based Milks

With such a variety of plant-based milks available, gone are the days when you would think you needed the dairy versions. For daily use and cooking, I am partial to nut milks. My personal favorite is unsweetened cashew milk. It is smooth and creamy, with a very neutral taste. But those who have nut allergies need not fear. There are many nut-free alternatives.

NUT MILKS

- Almond milk
- Cashew milk
- Hazelnut milk
- Macadamia milk

SEED, GRAIN, AND OTHER MILKS

- Coconut milk
- Flaxseed milk
- Hemp seed milk
- Oat milk
- Pea milk
- Rice milk
- Soy milk

Other Baking Items

Having these items on hand will make baking and preparing meals easy.

- Apple cider vinegar
- Baking powder
- Baking soda
- Coconut aminos or gluten-free soy sauce
- Lemon juice (preferably from fresh lemons)
- Nutritional yeast
- Sea salt
- Vanilla extract
- Vegan chocolate chips

Tools and Equipment

Cleaning up isn't fun, and thus I try to keep my kitchen tools and equipment to a minimum while cooking. The following list includes items I use most frequently when preparing the recipes in this book.

TOOLS

- **Large and small whisks**—For most of my recipes a whisk does the job just as well as a stand mixer and is much easier to clean and store.
- **Measuring cups and measuring spoons**—I have two sets of each, one for wet and one for dry.
- **Metal and rubber spatulas**
- **Mixing bowls**—small, medium, and large (ranging from 1½ to 3 quarts or liters)
- **Sharp knives and cutting boards**
- **Vegetable peeler**
- **Wooden spoons**

POTS AND PANS

- **Frying pans/skillets (small and large)**
- **Saucepans (small and large)**
- **Stock or soup pots**

EQUIPMENT

Both a food processor and a high-speed (variable) blender are often used in plant-based cooking. In some cases it is possible to use one instead of the other. I understand that these small appliances are an investment, but I highly recommend that you have these small appliances and kitchen tools.

- **Food processor**—An 11-cup size is a nice middle-of-the-road option.
- **High-speed (variable) blender**—The more powerful, the better. This will really help blend smooth, velvety sauces and soups and ensure your smoothies are always well combined.
- **Salad spinner**—This is a must for the perfect green salad. Spinners can usually be purchased for less than $20. I use mine daily. Removing the excess moisture from your greens before dressing them allows the dressing to stick to the leaves and not run to the bottom of the salad bowl.

BAKING

- **Baking sheets 13 x 18 x 1-inch**
- **8 x 8-inch baking dish**
- **13 x 9-inch baking dish**
- **Loaf pan 5¼ x 9 x 2¾-inch (1½-quart)**
- **Standard 12-cup muffin tin**
- **24-cup mini muffin tin**
Parchment paper

CHAPTER 2

Processes, Helpful Hints, *and* Staple Recipes

Processes, Techniques, and How-tos

These processes are used throughout the cookbook.

SOAKING NUTS

This process serves a dual purpose. It prepares the nuts to be broken down into creamy deliciousness, while at the same time neutralizing the phytic acid and enzyme inhibitors that are responsible for the digestive discomfort many people have when consuming nuts and beans. Because phytic acid and enzyme inhibitors are released during soaking, be sure to rinse the nuts well with fresh water after soaking to eliminate any trace elements of the digestive inhibitors.

To soak nuts, I use one of two methods.

Quick Soak Place the nuts in a glass bowl and cover with boiling water. Let the nuts soak for about 30 minutes or until soft and tender (or longer if specified in the recipe). Before use, rinse and drain the nuts to remove the digestive inhibitors that were released.

Overnight Soak If time allows, you can soak the nuts overnight. Place the nuts in a bowl and cover with cold water. Cover with a paper towel and refrigerate for about 8 hours. Before use, rinse and drain the nuts.

SAUTÉING WITHOUT OIL

Fat is not a bad thing. In fact, it is one of the three macronutrients—fat, carbohydrates, and proteins—required by the human body. That being said, it is best to get as much of your fat macronutrients from a *whole food*. Oils are fats but they are processed and thus not whole foods. Because of this, some of my recipes call for a minimal amount of oil while sautéing if I have determined that completely removing the oil will have a negative effect on the outcome of the dish. In an effort to reduce overall dietary oil consumption, I offer the option in many of my recipes to sauté with water or vegetable broth as an alternative. I have found that ceramic-coated, nonstick pans work well with this method:

• Add 1 to 2 tablespoons of water or broth to a pan, then place over heat. Once the water or broth is warm, add the ingredients as called for in the recipe. Add additional water or broth 1 tablespoon at a time, as often as needed to cook the food. Stir frequently to avoid burning.

WASHING FRUIT AND VEGETABLES

I don't buy bottled fruit and vegetable wash from the store. I find it expensive and I believe it leaves an aftertaste on my produce. Instead I buy an economy-size bottle of distilled white vinegar. I keep a spray bottle of it by the sink for washing fruit.

Gluten-free note: Most distilled white vinegar is gluten-free since it is made from apples, grapes, corn, or rice. As always, check the label before you buy.

Washing fruit: To wash a single piece of fruit, like an apple or pear, spray it with the pure distilled white vinegar. Clean the fruit by rubbing the dirt off with your hands and rinse thoroughly before consuming. To wash berries, place them in a strainer. Spray the berries with the pure distilled white vinegar

and toss a few times to be sure all berries are coated. Let the berries sit for a few minutes, then rinse thoroughly by gently shaking under running cold water. Drain before use.

Washing vegetables: To clean lettuce or other vegetables, add ⅓ cup to ½ cup vinegar to a medium mixing bowl and add cold water to fill. Place the vegetables in the bowl and mix them around in the vinegar water, making sure that they are all submerged. Let the vegetables soak for a few minutes, rinse well, and drain, or use a salad spinner where appropriate.

Storing fresh herbs: I love having fresh herbs on hand to use in recipes. To extend their shelf life, cut the bottom tips off the stems (about ½ inch) and place the herbs upright in a glass that is partially filled (about 2 inches) with filtered water. Use a produce bag to cover the top of the herbs, but be sure the bag is tented and not tightly fitted, to allow air to circulate around the herbs. This method will often extend the life of herbs by two weeks or more.

Freezing Bananas: I'm one of those people who can only eat bananas at a specific ripeness phase. For me, a little bit of green and no spots! I used to feel guilty about throwing away all those overripe bananas. Then I discovered freezing them. Plus, frozen bananas make an amazing whole food sweetener. Once ripe bananas have dark brown spots and become soft, they increase in sweetness and antioxidants. I use frozen bananas as a sweetener for my smoothies and, in a pinch, if a recipe calls for ripe banana.

To freeze, simply *peel* your very ripe bananas, place them in an airtight container or freezer-safe plastic bag, and store in the freezer for three months.

Skinning tomatoes: If you're using fresh tomatoes, bring a large pot of water to a boil. Score the bottom of the tomatoes with an "X" through the layer of skin. Place the tomatoes in the hot water for 1 minute. Remove and place them in an ice water bath for about 2 minutes, until they're cool. Remove the tomatoes from the water and peel them. The skin should come off with little effort.

Staple Recipes

Roasted Garlic

Makes 1 bulb roasted garlic

Prep time: 1 minute   **Cook time**: 35 minutes

1 bulb garlic

1 to 2 teaspoons olive oil

> **NOTE**
> – I use a toaster oven when I roast garlic, but a regular oven can be used too.

1. Preheat the oven to 400°F.

2. Slice off the top of the garlic bulb, about one-fifth of it, removing the tips of all the garlic cloves. Drizzle the olive oil onto the remaining four-fifths, so that the olive oil sinks into the cloves. Wrap the bulb in foil to prevent it from drying out when roasting. Place it on a baking sheet or directly on the oven rack and roast for 35 to 40 minutes.

3. When the roasting is complete, remove the foil-wrapped garlic bulb from the oven and carefully (so as not to burn yourself) open the foil. Allow to cool enough to handle with bare hands (about 15 minutes). To remove the roasted cloves, squeeze them from the base of the bulb. Each clove will easily slide out of its skin. Leftover roasted cloves may be stored in an airtight container in the refrigerator for up to 3 days.

Flax Egg

Makes 1 flax egg

This recipe will produce a gelatinous substance that is akin to an egg. An ideal replacement for eggs in baked goods, it is not recommended for dishes such as scrambled eggs. I use *golden* flax-seed meal as I find that it has a less earthy flavor than brown flax seed.

Prep time: 1 minute   **Cook time:** none

1 tablespoon golden
flaxseed meal

3 tablespoons water

To make a basic flax egg, combine the golden flaxseed meal with the water in a small bowl. Mix the ingredients together and set aside for 5 minutes before use.

> *A note about making and using flax egg:* While you will find flax eggs used in many recipes in this book, please read the instructions in each recipe. Some use plant-based milk or even coffee instead of water to add a special note or flavor accent to dishes.

Cashew Cream

Makes 1 cup

This recipe makes a basic cashew cream that is similar to heavy cream. To make a lighter cream, add one tablespoon of water at a time until the desired consistency is achieved.

Prep time: 5 minutes   **Cook time:** none

1 cup raw cashews, soaked
(see page 17)

³/₄ cup filtered water

After soaking the cashews, rinse, drain, and transfer them to a high-speed blender. Add the water and pulse until the nuts are broken into small pieces. Blend on medium speed until combined, then high speed until smooth, about 3 minutes. Pause to scrape down the sides of the blender as necessary.

Coconut Butter/Manna

Makes ³/₄ cup coconut butter

When the addition of coconut flavor is welcome, use coconut butter/manna as you would a nut butter. Spread it on toast, Blueberry Banana Bread (page 120), or use it in Pure Piña Colada Bars (page 216).

Prep time: 5 to 8 minutes   **Cook time:** none

3 rounded cups shredded or flaked dehydrated unsweetened coconut (not desiccated or finely ground)

¼ teaspoon sea salt, or more or less to taste (optional)

Place the coconut in a food processor. Pulse a few times to break the coconut into smaller pieces, then blend until the butter is smooth and has reached the desired texture. Pause as necessary to scrape down the sides of the container. If your processor is getting overheated, it is fine to stop and give it a rest. It will not affect the coconut butter. After processing, the coconut butter will initially be more fluid as a result of the heat from the processing but as it cools, it will firm up. Store in an airtight container in the refrigerator for up to 1 month.

> **NOTE**
> - If more coconut butter or manna is desired, add shredded or flaked coconut accordingly. The processing time will increase proportionately.

CHAPTER 3

Breakfasts

Double Chocolate Chip Pancakes

Makes 8 to 9 four-inch pancakes

Let's face it: Pancakes aren't the easiest recipe to convert into a plant-based and gluten-free dish. The bulk of the traditional recipe consists of eggs, milk, and flour—and lots of sugar. Just the right blend of gluten-free flours gives these pancakes that pillowy, light chew of traditional pancakes, while maintaining a moist, soft center—and all without the use of oil! The addition of cocoa and warm melted chocolate makes them a decadent, guilt-free breakfast delight. And talk about kid-friendly!

Prep time: 10 minutes **Cook time**: 10 minutes

1 ¼ cups unsweetened plant-based milk (I use cashew milk)

2 teaspoons apple cider vinegar

¾ cup almond meal

½ cup white rice flour

½ cup tapioca flour or tapioca starch

⅓ cup unsweetened cocoa powder

¼ cup mini vegan chocolate chips (such as Enjoy Life brand)

3 tablespoons coconut sugar

2 teaspoons baking powder

¼ teaspoon finely ground sea salt (rounded)

¼ cup unsweetened applesauce

1 teaspoon vanilla extract

> **NOTES**
> - Pancakes can be kept refrigerated in an airtight container for 2 to 3 days or 2 months in the freezer. To reheat, place the pancake in a toaster or a toaster oven for 2 to 3 minutes.
> - See my technique for measuring gluten-free flour (page 12) to ensure consistent measurements.

1. In a small mixing bowl, stir together the plant-based milk and apple cider vinegar. Set aside for 5 minutes to become a light "buttermilk."

2. In a medium mixing bowl, place the almond meal, white rice flour, tapioca flour, cocoa powder, chocolate chips, coconut sugar, baking powder, and salt. Stir to combine evenly.

3. Add the applesauce and vanilla to the milk mixture and stir to combine.

4. Add the wet ingredients to the dry ingredients and stir together. Set aside and allow the batter to thicken while preheating a griddle or pan for 5 minutes.

5. Heat a nonstick griddle or pan (I use a griddle) over medium heat. The pan is ready when a few droplets of water dance when dripped on the pan. Using a ¼ cup measure, pour the measured batter on the griddle and gently spread the batter into a circle about ¼-inch thick with a diameter of 4 inches.

6. Cook for about 3 to 4 minutes or until the edge of each pancake becomes dull. There will not be as many bubbles as in traditional pancakes. Flip the pancake and cook about 2 additional minutes. To serve, drizzle with maple syrup or your favorite nut butter.

NOTES

Substitutions: ½ cup quick-cooking oats may be used in place of the quinoa. Water and cooking time may need to be increased if using the stovetop for oats.

Nut-free option: Omit the chopped nuts and replace the cashew milk with a plant-based milk not derived from nuts.

Apple Pie Quinoa Breakfast Bowl

Servings: 1

When the leaves start turning their fall colors and the wind starts brushing the trees, I reach for my sweaters and my morning comfort foods. I started making this breakfast bowl when apples came into season, but it became a staple through winter because nothing says warm and cozy like a bowl of hot cereal laced with sweet apples, cinnamon, and brown sugar. Plus, it's best to start your day with a breakfast with plant protein and other nutrients that also warm your soul. You can have it ready in five minutes, so you won't be late for work!

Prep time: 3 minutes   **Cook time:** 2 minutes

1 medium apple

1 small (or two-thirds of a medium) ripe banana, mashed

⅛ teaspoon finely ground sea salt

⅛ teaspoon cinnamon, to taste

1 teaspoon coconut sugar, to taste

1 tablespoon chopped walnuts or pecans

⅓ cup quinoa hot cereal flakes

½ cup cold water

3 tablespoons cashew milk (or other plant-based milk) to pour on top (optional)

1. Cut the apple in half and dice one half or until you have ¼ cup. Set aside. Slice the remaining half and set aside.

2. Mash the banana in a bowl and mix in the salt until the banana mixture has a buttery texture. Stir in the cinnamon, coconut sugar, walnuts, and diced apple.

3. Add the quinoa flakes and water to the banana mixture and stir to combine. Microwave for 2 minutes on high power, stirring every 45 seconds or 1 minute. Alternatively, ingredients may be combined in a small saucepan and cooked on the stovetop. Bring to a boil and simmer for an additional 1 to 2 minutes for the quinoa flakes and 3 to 4 minutes for oats.

4. After 2 minutes, remove from the microwave and stir. Top the warm cereal with the apple slices and the remaining banana or toppings of choice. Pour the cashew milk over the cereal, if desired, and enjoy!

Eggless Chickpea Scramble

Servings: 3

When you're craving a hearty homestyle breakfast, nothing satisfies like a plate piled high with this piping-hot chickpea scramble, my Portobello Bacon (page 30), and a stack of gluten-free toast with my Coconut Butter/Manna (page 21).

Prep time: 5 minutes   **Cook time:** 8 minutes

1 (15-ounce) can chickpeas

2 tablespoons chopped green onion, white part only but green parts reserved

½ teaspoon dried cilantro

¼ teaspoon granulated garlic

¼ teaspoon finely ground sea salt

¼ teaspoon chile powder

dash black pepper

¾ teaspoon nutritional yeast or more, if desired

NOTES

- If you enjoy the sulfuric smell of cooked eggs, add black salt in addition to sea salt or instead of it.

- Additional amounts of chickpea fluid may be added if you prefer a wetter scramble.

---

1. Drain the canned chickpeas in a colander over a bowl to reserve the aquafaba, the liquid in the can. Set aside the aquafaba and pour the drained chickpeas into another small or medium mixing bowl.

2. Roughly mash the chickpeas into ⅛ to ¼ inch pieces.

3. Add the chopped onion, cilantro, granulated garlic, sea salt, chile powder, and black pepper to the chickpeas and stir to combine.

4. Lightly grease a medium skillet with a high-temperature oil such as avocado oil. You can also use a teaspoon or two of water for an oil-free version. Place the skillet over medium heat. Add the chickpea mixture and lightly sauté, stirring occasionally, every 3 to 5 minutes, until small pieces of chickpeas start to turn golden brown.

5. Stir in the nutritional yeast. Then add 4 tablespoons of the chickpea fluid, one tablespoon at a time, stirring the chickpea mixture after each additional tablespoon. Continue sautéing until the desired level of wetness is achieved. Serve immediately. Leftovers may be stored in an airtight container in the refrigerator for 2 to 3 days and reheated in a skillet on the stovetop over medium heat for 3 to 4 minutes when ready to eat.

Portobello Bacon

Servings: 6

Most people don't realize that what they love about bacon is not the taste of the meat, but the way it is made. The chewy texture covered in a sweet, spicy tang, paired up with a bit of smokiness—*that's* bacon. This mushroom-based recipe will have your die-hard bacon lovers fist-bumping you as they reach for another round. Plus, it's low in fat as well as nutrient-dense. A perfect match for my Eggless Chickpea Scramble (page 29). Not to mention, your BLT just made a new best friend.

Prep time: 10 minutes   **Cook time:** 22 to 25 minutes

3 medium/large portobello mushroom caps

¼ cup coconut aminos

1 teaspoon prepared mustard

½ teaspoon dried chives

¼ teaspoon finely ground sea salt, plus more for seasoning while baking

⅛ teaspoon onion powder

⅛ teaspoon paprika, plus more for seasoning while baking

dash black pepper

1. Preheat the oven to 425°F. Line a baking sheet with parchment paper.

2. Clean the mushrooms (see page 201 for instructions). Once clean, pull off the stems and use a teaspoon to gently scrape out the gills. Discard the stems and gills. Using a sharp knife, slice the cleaned mushroom caps in ⅛- to ¼-inch-wide strips. Set aside.

3. In a small mixing bowl combine the remaining ingredients except the mushrooms and mix well.

4. Gently toss the mushrooms in the marinade and place the slices on the baking sheet. Place the baking sheet in the preheated oven and bake for 10 minutes.

5. After 10 minutes, turn the strips over and sprinkle with additional paprika and salt. Return them to the oven and continue baking for an additional 12 to 15 minutes depending on desired level of crispiness. Remove from the oven and serve immediately. Leftovers may be stored in an airtight container in the refrigerator for 3 to 4 days and reheated on a baking sheet in a regular oven or a toaster oven at 425°F for 5 to 10 minutes when ready to eat.

Maple Drizzle Donuts

It could be argued that donut cravings have helped sell more coffee and tea than any other food. But a hankering for these little treats doesn't mean you have to be weighed down with all the refined sugar, oil, and (ultimately) regret. These donuts have a moist and tender cake with just the right amount of natural sweetness to get you through your morning or a satisfying afternoon tea.

Prep time: 15 minutes   **Cook time:** 10 minutes

1 tablespoon golden flaxseed meal

3 tablespoons unsweetened plant-based milk

½ cup sweet white sorghum flour

½ cup almond meal

½ cup gluten-free oat flour

⅓ cup coconut sugar

3 tablespoons arrowroot

1 teaspoon baking powder

¼ teaspoon finely ground sea salt

½ cup cashew or almond milk

3 tablespoons smoothly mashed ripe banana

2 teaspoons vanilla extract

1½ teaspoons apple cider vinegar

⅓ cup maple syrup

1 teaspoon lemon juice

¼ teaspoon vanilla extract

1½ teaspoons arrowroot

1½ teaspoons water

1. Preheat the oven to 350°F. If you're not using a nonstick pan, lightly grease the donut receptacles (no longer oil free).

2. In a small mixing bowl stir together the golden flaxseed meal and 3 tablespoons of plant-based milk. Set the flax egg aside for 5 minutes.

3. In a medium mixing bowl, combine the sorghum flour, almond meal, gluten-free oat flour, coconut sugar, arrowroot, baking powder, and sea salt. Be sure not to pack the flours when measuring. Stir together the dry ingredients. I like to use a hand whisk to mix these ingredients thoroughly.

4. Stir the flax egg. Add the cashew milk, mashed banana, vanilla, and apple cider vinegar. Stir together well.

5. Add the wet ingredients to the dry ingredients and mix together well. I like to use a hand whisk for this step.

6. Fill 6 baking cavities of the donut baking pan, until slightly below the rim of the cavity. Do not overfill. Place the pan in the oven and bake for 10 to 12 minutes. If you are using a pan with 9 or 12 baking

(continued on page 33)

- This recipe uses a donut baking pan.

- If you serve these donuts with the maple drizzle, they are best enjoyed immediately. The donuts will keep for a few days in an airtight container, either at room temperature or in the refrigerator, but the drizzle tends to melt over time. Alternatively, the drizzle may be stored separately and reserved for serving.

- See my technique for measuring gluten-free flour (page 12) to ensure consistent measurements.

cavities, you may want to place a tablespoon of water in the empty cavities to prevent them from burning or warping.

7. Remove the pan from the oven when a toothpick inserted into one of the donuts comes out clean. Place the donut pan on a cooling rack and allow the donuts to cool in the pan for 2 to 3 minutes. Remove the donuts from the pan and allow them to continue cooling on the rack for 10 to 15 minutes.

8. While the donuts cool, make the drizzle. Place the maple syrup in a small saucepan and bring to a simmer. Add the lemon juice and vanilla and allow the sauce to simmer for an additional 1 to 2 minutes.

9. In a small bowl, whisk together the arrowroot and water to create a slurry. Whisk the slurry into the simmering mixture until smooth. Continue to rapidly whisk the mixture until it begins to thicken and appears to have a sheen, about 1 to 2 minutes. Remove the pan from the heat and allow the mixture to continue to thicken for approximately 5 minutes.

10. Once the mixture has thickened to the consistency of thick syrup and the donuts have completely cooled, drizzle the syrup over the donuts. The donuts may be stored in an airtight container for 3 to 5 days. I recommend keeping them in the refrigerator if you're storing them for more than 1 day.

Fresh Face Smoothie

Makes 3 eight-ounce servings

This creamsicle-colored, palate-pleasing, nutrient-packed glass of goodness is my go-to smoothie. I loaded this recipe with ingredients that are a blast of vitamins, minerals, and proteins. Carrots, which are high in beta-carotene, an antioxidant converted to vitamin A inside the body, help to repair skin tissue. Plus they serve up that pretty orange hue. The golden flaxseed meal is a great source of omega-3s, which help protect your skin, heart, and brain. And along with the pear, the flaxseed meal contributes to the smoothie's creamy and thick texture. It's like rejuvenation in a glass!

Prep time: 5 minutes   **Cook time:** none

1 cup unsweetened cashew milk or other mild-tasting plant-based milk for a nut-free option

2 tablespoons golden flaxseed meal

1 ripe pear, cored and quartered

1 medium carrot, peeled and roughly chopped

1 large extra-ripe banana, frozen

1 scoop/serving vanilla plant-based, gluten-free protein powder

1 teaspoon vanilla extract

1 teaspoon apple cider vinegar

1 cup crushed ice

1. Place the cashew milk and golden flaxseed meal in a blender. Stir to combine and allow to soak for 3 to 4 minutes while adding the additional ingredients. This makes a nice thickening agent for your smoothie.

2. Blend on high speed until creamy and smooth, about 1 to 2 minutes. If you are not using a high-speed blender, additional time may be necessary to thoroughly blend the carrot.

3. Turn the blender off and taste the smoothie with a spoon. If it tastes too rich, add more water or ice and blend. If it's not sweet enough, add more frozen banana and blend. When the smoothie is to taste, pour it into a glass and enjoy.

- I use golden flaxseed meal in my smoothies, rather than brown flaxseed meal. I find it to have a milder flavor that pairs better with a variety of ingredients.

- I recommend using a high-quality, organic, plant-based, gluten-free protein powder with no added sugar, such as Garden of Life or Vega. While protein powder is not a whole food and should not serve as a dietary substitute, quality protein powders can be a viable option for supplementing when the alternative is something less healthy.

- I drink one glass immediately to enjoy maximum nutrient benefit and then place my blender container in the freezer to make the remaining servings extra cold and thick! The freezer also slows the process of the nutrients breaking down, though it is best to consume the juice as soon as possible within a 24-hour period.

Strawberry Banana Overnight Chia Oats

Servings: 2 (1 $^2/_3$ cups total)

Mornings can be rough. Sometimes you don't even have time for a five-minute breakfast. Eating in a rush usually means you are not eating well—but it doesn't have to be that way. These tasty overnight oats are super-satisfying and will be waiting for you in the morning, ready to supply you with a dose of protein and omega-3s. And if breakfast in bed is the order of the morning, even better—no crumbs!

Prep time: 5 minutes   **Cook time**: none

$^1/_2$ cup mashed ripe banana

1 tablespoon lemon juice

$^1/_2$ cup mashed strawberries

1 teaspoon vanilla

1 teaspoon maple syrup (optional)

1 tablespoon chia seeds

$^1/_2$ cup gluten-free rolled oats

$^1/_2$ cup unsweetened plant-based milk (I use cashew milk, but then the recipe is no longer nut-free)

pinch finely ground sea salt (optional)

1. In a jar, place all ingredients in the order they appear. It is important to mix the lemon juice in with the banana first, to help prevent the banana from turning brown overnight. Once all ingredients have been added, put the lid on the jar and shake to combine. Place in the refrigerator overnight or for 6 to 8 hours.

2. In the morning, pour the desired amount into a bowl or a parfait glass and top or layer with toppings such as berries, nuts, or seeds. Blueberries and walnuts are two of my favorite additions.

NOTES

- Alternative refined sugar–free sweeteners like coconut nectar, coconut sugar, or date sugar can replace the maple syrup.

- If you prefer a no-added-sugar option, omit the maple syrup and add 2 to 3 additional tablespoons of mashed ripe banana.

Mocha Pumpkin Mini Muffins

Servings: 24

Combining pumpkin, coffee, and chocolate may sound a little odd, but recipe development is partly about testing the limits of ingredients and not missing any diamonds in the rough. You can't lose with the blending of chocolate and coffee—but pumpkin? When combined in these muffins (or cookies) it takes on a natural caramel quality that is unmatched.

Prep time: 15 minutes   **Cook time:** 13 minutes

3 tablespoons golden flaxseed meal

¹⁄₂ cup very strong coffee

3 cups almond meal

¹⁄₃ cup coconut sugar

³⁄₄ teaspoon baking soda

¹⁄₂ teaspoon finely ground sea salt

¹⁄₄ teaspoon cinnamon

³⁄₄ cup vegan mini chocolate chips, plus ¹⁄₄ cup vegan mini chocolate chips (for chocolate drizzle, if desired)

²⁄₃ cup mashed pumpkin (preferably canned, for lower moisture content)

1 tablespoon vanilla extract

> **NOTE**
> – See my technique for measuring gluten-free flour (page 12) to ensure consistent measurements.

1. Preheat the oven to 350°F. Line a muffin tin with paper liners.

2. In a small mixing bowl, stir or whisk together the golden flaxseed meal and coffee. Set aside.

3. In a medium or large mixing bowl, whisk together the almond meal, coconut sugar, baking soda, sea salt, and cinnamon. Stir in ¾ cup of mini vegan chocolate chips.

4. Add the pumpkin and vanilla to the flax egg mixture and stir well. Add the wet ingredients to the dry ingredients and combine well with a wooden spoon. This may take a minute or two as the dough is very dense.

5. Using a melon ball scoop (about 1 tablespoon) or a tablespoon, place 2 scoops of dough into each cup in the mini muffin tin. Using your fingers, press the dough into the cup to fill the cups. Flatten the tops. Bake for 13 minutes until the tops are slightly firm to the touch and the edges are just beginning to brown.

6. After baking, place the muffin tin on a cooling rack and let stand for 10 minutes. Remove the muffins and place them directly on the cooling rack to continue to cool.

7. As the muffins cool, make the drizzle, if desired. Melt the remaining chocolate chips in the microwave or on the stovetop in a pan or double boiler. Using a teaspoon, drizzle on top of the cooled muffins. These may be stored in an airtight container at room temperature or in the refrigerator. They keep well for about 5 to 7 days. They may also be frozen for 2 to 3 months. Remove them from the freezer to thaw for a few hours before eating.

Variation

Alternatively, you can make these into cookies. Follow the instructions through step 4. Then, scoop 1 tablespoon of dough into your palm. Roll it into a ball and then flatten into a ¼-inch-thick disk. Bake at 350°F on a parchment-lined baking sheet for 8 minutes until they begin to brown and crisp around the edges. Remove the baking sheet from the oven and let the cookies cool on the baking sheet for 5 to 10 minutes. Transfer the cookies to a cooling rack and let them cool completely.

Apple Carrot Cake Muffins

Servings: 12

These sweet treats are perfect for breakfast or as dessert at a holiday gathering. The ideal blend of fruits and baking spices, these muffins are like holding autumn in the palm of your hand, and the scent of them baking will draw people into your kitchen.

Prep time: 15 minutes   **Cook time:** 25 minutes

2 tablespoons golden flaxseed meal

⅓ cup unsweetened, mild-tasting plant-based milk, like cashew or almond

2 cups almond meal

1 cup gluten-free rolled oats

¼ cup arrowroot

¼ cup coconut sugar

1 teaspoon cinnamon

½ teaspoon ground nutmeg

½ teaspoon ground ginger

¾ teaspoon baking soda

½ teaspoon finely ground sea salt

1 large extra-ripe banana, mashed, about ½ cup

2 teaspoons vanilla extract

2 teaspoons apple cider vinegar

1 large apple, peeled, cored, and diced into ¼-inch cubes, about 1 cup

¾ cup grated carrot

> **NOTE**
> – See my technique for measuring gluten-free flour (page 12) to ensure consistent measurements.

1. Preheat the oven to 350°F. Lightly grease or line a muffin tin with paper liners.

2. In a small bowl, stir or whisk together the golden flaxseed meal and plant-based milk. Set aside.

3. In a medium or large mixing bowl, stir or whisk together the almond meal, gluten-free oats, arrowroot, coconut sugar, cinnamon, nutmeg, ginger, baking soda, and sea salt.

4. Add the mashed banana, vanilla, and apple cider vinegar to the flax egg and whisk together.

5. Add the wet ingredients to the dry ingredients and combine well with a wooden spoon. This may take a minute or two as the batter is very dense. Gently stir in the apple and carrot. If the batter is too thick to combine, add 1 to 2 tablespoons of plant-based milk to loosen.

6. Using a standard ice cream scoop or a spoon, place about ¼ cup of batter in each muffin cup. Since the batter is thick, you will need to press it down into the muffin cups with your fingers or the back of a spoon. Bake for approximately 25 minutes, until the muffins begin to show brownish peaks, and a toothpick inserted comes out clean.

7. Remove the muffin tin from the oven and cool the muffins in the tin for 15 minutes, then remove from the tin and place on a cooling rack. They will keep for 1 week in an airtight container in the refrigerator.

Sweet Golden Pancakes

Servings: 8 four-inch pancakes

Some days just call for pancakes. When the snow falls atop the hills of our town in Virginia, the morning call of duty is a hot pot of coffee, stacks of these pancakes, and a platter of my Portobello Bacon (page 30). Pull up a chair, grab a plate, and watch the snow fall.

Prep time: 10 minutes   **Cook time:** 8 minutes

1 cup unsweetened plant-based milk (I use cashew milk)

¼ cup unsweetened applesauce

2 teaspoons lemon juice

1 teaspoon vanilla extract

1 cup almond meal

¾ cup white rice flour

½ cup tapioca flour or starch

3 tablespoons coconut sugar

1½ teaspoons baking soda

¼ teaspoon finely ground sea salt

NOTE
- See my technique for measuring gluten-free flour (page 12) to ensure consistent measurements.

1. In a small mixing bowl, stir or whisk together the plant-based milk, applesauce, lemon juice, and vanilla. Set aside.

2. In a medium mixing bowl, combine the almond meal, white rice flour, tapioca flour, coconut sugar, baking soda, and salt.

3. Add the wet ingredients to the dry and stir or whisk together. Once thoroughly combined, set aside and allow the batter to thicken for about 5 to 10 minutes.

4. Heat a nonstick griddle or pan over medium heat. The pan is ready when a couple of water droplets dance when dripped on the pan. Using a ¼-cup measure, pour the measured batter on the griddle, and gently spread the batter into a circle about ¼ inch thick with a diameter of 4 inches. Allow to cook until the edge becomes dull, about 3 to 5 minutes, depending on the size of the pancake. There will not be as many bubbles as there are in traditional pancakes. Flip the pancakes and cook about 2 additional minutes. Serve with maple syrup, nut butters, or fruit topping.

Tip: Pancakes can be kept refrigerated in an airtight container for 2 to 3 days or in the freezer for 2 months. To reheat, place the pancake in a toaster or a toaster oven for 2 to 3 minutes.

NOTES

- Make this dish nut-free by replacing the walnuts with sprouted pumpkin seeds or sunflower seeds. Also substitute a mild-tasting nut-free, plant-based milk, such as oat milk, for the cashew milk.

  Helpful hint: Amounts can easily be increased to serve this dish as a side.

Sweet and Comforting Veggie Porridge

Servings: 1

Veggies for breakfast? You bet. And talk about starting your day off right! Spinach and carrots span the vegetable rainbow nicely, while walnuts offer protein and healthy fats. Plus, the raisins deliver a delightful pop of sweetness, and the flaxseed-cashew sauce provides omega-3s while it blankets the dish with subtle nutmeg and cinnamon. Beyond breakfast, this would make a great side dish at any meal.

Prep time: 5 minutes   **Cook time:** 5 minutes

1 tablespoon golden flaxseed meal

3 tablespoons unsweetened cashew milk

2 cups fresh baby spinach leaves (washed and dried)

⅓ cup grated carrot

¼ cup golden raisins

1 tablespoon chopped walnuts

freshly ground nutmeg, to taste

ground cinnamon, to taste

stevia, if more sweetness is desired

1. In a small bowl, mix the golden flaxseed and cashew milk. Set aside.

2. Place 1 teaspoon filtered water in the bottom of a small saucepan over medium-low heat. Add the spinach, grated carrot, raisins, and chopped walnuts to the saucepan. Gently toss the mixture until the spinach and carrot begin to lose some of their crunchy texture but before the vegetables begin to wilt, about 2 to 3 minutes. Gently toss with tongs to avoid damaging the vegetables.

3. While the mixture is cooking, add the nutmeg and cinnamon to the flaxseed–cashew milk mixture and stir to combine. If you prefer a sweeter dish, you can add stevia to taste as well.

4. Add the flaxseed–cashew milk mixture to the saucepan and gently toss the vegetables with the tongs. Remove the pan from the heat immediately and serve.

Healing and Revitalizing Detox Juice

Makes 1 to 2 servings

There are two schools of thought on juicing: One believes it's a very healthy way to get your nutrients. The other believes that removing the flesh and skin puts the fruit and vegetables in a concentrated form and is not what the body was meant to digest. I don't think it has to be all or nothing. There are times and perhaps seasons of life where juicing is a viable alternative. When I was recovering from major spine surgery, I wanted to flood my body with nutrients. My goal was to optimize the healing process and keep my immune system strong. I did this by drinking this juice and eating whole food, plant-based meals. Alternatively, I have provided a recipe for a smoothie that retains the flesh of the fruit and vegetables. Pick your potion!

Prep time: 5 minutes   **Cook time:** none

1 carrot, peeled

½ medium zucchini

½ medium cucumber

3 leaves baby bok choy

1 handful romaine lettuce

1 red apple, a sweet variety such as Honeycrisp

1 lime, peeled

Wash all ingredients and cut in an appropriate size to fit in your juicer tube. Run all ingredients through a masticating juicer. Stir well and pour the juice into a glass. Cover the glass with plastic wrap to seal and preserve nutrients and place in the freezer for 10 minutes. Remove and immediately enjoy!

DETOX SMOOTHIE

Peel the carrot, zucchini, cucumber, apple, and lime. Place the peeled fruits and vegetables in a high-speed blender with ¼ cup of filtered water and 1 cup of ice. Ingredients may need to be pushed down with a tamper while initially blending. Additional water or ice may be added to reach desired consistency.

Nutrition Notes

Every ingredient in this recipe brings a wealth of nutrients to your body.

CARROTS are loaded with antioxidants. Vitamin A brings health to your eyes and rejuvenation to your skin cells.

ZUCCHINI offers significant amounts of vitamin B6, C, K, riboflavin, and folate. It also boasts antioxidants and anti-inflammatories.

CUCUMBER is a good source of fiber, potassium, and magnesium

BABY BOK CHOY is high in vitamins A, C, and K, and is an excellent source of calcium, magnesium, potassium, and iron.

ROMAINE LETTUCE is a great source of vitamins A, C, K, and folate.

APPLES are filled with phytochemicals that help rid your body of toxins and relieve strain on the liver.

LIMES, in addition to providing a host of vitamins, are particularly high in flavonoids that promote healthy digestion.

CHAPTER 4

Soups, Salads, *and* Dressings

Quinoa Leek Bisque

Servings: 4

This bisque pairs a subtle nutty taste with a creamy texture so velvety smooth, no one will guess it's dairy-free. Decidedly filling, it provides warmth and comfort on the coldest of days.

Prep time: 15 minutes   **Cook time**: 20 minutes

1 tablespoon olive oil (or sauté in vegetable broth or water for oil-free option, page 17)

2 fresh leeks, white part only, halved lengthwise and sliced into half moons

2 large cloves fresh garlic, minced

1 stalk celery, chopped

1/2 teaspoon finely ground sea salt

dash finely ground black pepper

1/2 cup raw cashews, soaked

3 cups vegetable broth, divided

1/2 cup uncooked sprouted quinoa, rinsed

1 tablespoon red wine vinegar or lemon juice

unsweetened plant-based milk (may be used for thinning, if desired)

grated carrot or chopped chives for garnish, if desired

> **NOTE**
> - Soaking cashews is required prior to starting this recipe. See page 17 for quick-soak or overnight-soak instructions.

1. Heat the oil in a large saucepan over medium heat. Add the leeks, garlic, and celery. Add the salt and pepper, and sauté until the celery begins to appear translucent. Stir occasionally.

2. While the vegetables are sautéing, place the cashews in a blender with 1 cup vegetable broth. Blend on medium or medium-high until smooth, about 1 to 2 minutes. Set aside.

3. Add the quinoa to the sautéed vegetables in the saucepan and stir. Cook for 1 minute and then add the remaining 2 cups of vegetable broth and bring to a boil. Reduce to low heat and continue to cook for 15 minutes. Stir and remove from the heat. Allow to cool for 5 minutes.

4. Add the vegetable-quinoa mixture to the cashew cream in the blender. Depending on the size of your blender, this may need to be done in batches. Cover the blender with the lid, but leave the lid open a bit and hold it

with your hand. This will allow heat to escape, preventing pressure from building up. Pulse a couple of times to begin to break down the vegetables, then blend on medium or medium-high until smooth. Carefully remove the lid. Add the vinegar or lemon juice, cover, and blend until mixed. Alternatively, you can add the cashew cream to the saucepan and use an immersion blender for this step.

5. Serve the soup immediately, garnishing with grated carrot or chopped chives.

Tips: If a warmer serving temperature is desired, the soup can be placed back in the saucepan and heated. If a thinner consistency is desired, plant-based milk can be added to the soup in the blender or saucepan as well. I would not recommend adding more than ½ cup of plant-based milk as the flavor may become altered.

Simple Skillet Soup

Servings: 4

This soup makes a great addition to a weeknight meal any time of year, but it's an absolute lifesaver when you feel under the weather. One of the last things you want to do if you're fighting a cold is stand in the kitchen and cook, but that's when you need that home-cooked goodness the most. This soup is simple to prepare and yields a bowl full of antioxidants, plant-based protein, vitamins, and minerals to help cure what ails you. And it does a fine job of keeping you healthy too!

Prep time: 5 minutes **Cook time:** 35 minutes

1 teaspoon olive oil (or sauté in vegetable broth for oil-free option, page 17)

1 medium sweet onion chopped, about 1 cup

3 tablespoons minced fresh garlic

½ teaspoon dried oregano

½ teaspoon paprika

½ teaspoon finely ground sea salt

¼ teaspoon coarsely ground black pepper

1 quart vegetable broth

½ to ¾ cup fresh cilantro chopped

1 (15-ounce) can Great Northern beans, partially drained

1 (15-ounce) can black beans

1. Heat the olive oil in a large skillet or one with high sides (I used a 12" x 3" pan) over medium heat and sauté the onion and garlic for 5 minutes or until translucent and light brown. Stir in the oregano, paprika, salt, and black pepper. Sauté an additional 1–2 minutes.

2. Add the vegetable broth and stir, loosening any onion or garlic from the bottom of the pan. Raise the heat to medium-high, stir in the cilantro according to taste preferences, and bring to a gentle boil, about 5 to 7 minutes. Reduce heat to a simmer.

3. Drain one-quarter to half of the liquid from both cans of beans and add the beans to the pan. Bring the soup back up to a simmer. It will take about 5 minutes. Cook for 10 minutes then taste and adjust seasoning, if desired.

4. Remove the pan from the heat. Using a potato masher, gently mash the beans about 10 times, then stir. Most beans will remain whole while enough are mashed to thicken the soup. Return the pan to the heat and continue the rapid simmer for at least 5 minutes,

stirring periodically until desired consistency is reached. To achieve a thicker consistency, mash beans a few more times and cook an additional 10 to 15 minutes at a rapid simmer. Store in the refrigerator for 3 to 5 days in an airtight container.

NOTE

> **Serving option:** If you are in the mood for something a little heartier, an extended cooking time and a little extra mashing will yield a thicker soup (see step 4).

Rosemary Potato and Corn Chowder

Makes 5 to 6 one-cup servings

When the autumn harvest reaches its peak, this chowder will bring it to its fullest expression. Butternut squash, potato, corn, and onion serve as the hearty base, and thyme and rosemary deliver a rich, earthy component. The sweetness of the squash and corn is balanced against the savory flavors of the herbs and potatoes. This chowder is a belly-filling and body-satisfying meal to warm you from head to toe. It also reheats well for a quick meal after a long day at work.

Prep time: 10 minutes   **Cook time**: 30 minutes

1 teaspoon olive oil

1 medium sweet onion, diced (about 1 cup)

3 tablespoons minced garlic (about 5 fresh garlic cloves)

1 teaspoon finely ground sea salt, divided

1/2 teaspoon dried thyme

1/2 teaspoon dried rosemary

1/8 teaspoon ground cayenne, or to taste

1 1/2 cups butternut squash, peeled and cut in 1/2-inch cubes

1 pound white potatoes, peeled and chopped in 1/2-inch cubes (about 3 cups)

2 cups vegetable broth

1 cup unsweetened, mild-tasting plant-based milk (I like cashew, but recipe will no longer be nut-free)

2 teaspoons lemon juice

1 cup sweet corn, drained

> **NOTE**
> – For an oil-free version, replace the olive oil in the recipe with vegetable broth or water. See instructions for sautéing without oil on page 17.

1. In a 6-quart pan or large stockpot, heat the olive oil over medium heat. Add the onion, garlic, 1/4 teaspoon salt, thyme, rosemary, and cayenne. When adding the thyme and rosemary, crumble the herbs with your fingers. Sauté until the onion becomes translucent, about 5 to 6 minutes.

2. Add the squash, potatoes, and the remaining 3/4 teaspoon salt to pot. Stirring frequently, cook about 5 additional minutes or until the squash and potatoes soften. Then add the vegetable broth and milk. Bring the chowder to a boil and reduce to a simmer, stirring occasionally, until the squash and potatoes are fork-tender, about 15 to 20 minutes. Reduce the heat to low.

3. Remove 1 cup of the chowder from the pot and add it to a blender. Cover the blender with the lid, but leave the lid open a bit and hold it with your hand. This will allow heat to escape, preventing pressure from building. Or remove the center of the lid and cover it with a towel. Blend on high speed until smooth. Add the lemon juice and blend on high for a few seconds to incorporate. If a smoother chowder is desired, a second cup of soup may be blended until smooth.

4. Return the contents of the blender to the pan with the remaining chowder. Add the sweet corn and stir to combine. Leave the chowder on low heat for a couple minutes for the flavors to blend. Serve warm. Store in an airtight container in the refrigerator for several days or freeze for a couple of months. For reheating, place in a covered pan over medium-low heat and stir frequently until hot. If the chowder needs to be thinned, add 2 to 3 tablespoons of plant-based milk or vegetable broth.

Creamy Waldorf Salad

Talk about a culinary leap! Back in 1893 at New York's Waldorf Hotel, someone said, "I've got a great idea. It involves apples, celery, and mayonnaise!" It might've made people think twice, but what a creative notion. A sweet and savory dish that's light on its feet, this version makes a sensational appetizer or side salad, but is still substantial enough to serve over a bed of greens as a light meal. One of my favorite things about this salad is its flexibility. Like it on the sweet side? Add some coconut sugar to the dressing. More savory? Spice it up with a little extra garlic powder. Make it your own!

Prep time: 20 minutes   **Cook time:** None

1 cup raw cashews, soaked

1/2 cup unsweetened plant-based milk (I use cashew milk)

4 tablespoons lemon juice, divided

1 teaspoon apple cider vinegar

3/4 teaspoon finely ground sea salt

1/4 teaspoon prepared mustard

1/4 teaspoon granulated garlic (optional)

2 cups cored and chopped crisp sweet red apple, about 1/2-inch pieces (I use Gala apples)

1 cup halved red grapes

1/2 cup golden raisins

1/2 cup chopped pecans or walnuts

1/4 cup diced celery, 1/8- to 1/4-inch pieces

Boston or green leaf lettuce, for serving if desired

NOTE

– Soaking cashews is required prior to starting this recipe. See page 17 for quick-soak or overnight-soak instructions.

---

1. *To make the dressing:* Place the soaked cashews, plant-based milk, 2 tablespoons lemon juice, apple cider vinegar, salt, mustard, and garlic in a blender or food processor. Pulse a few times to chop the cashews. Blend on high speed until smooth, stopping periodically to scrape the sides.

2. *To make the salad:* Place the apple in a medium mixing bowl. Sprinkle the apple with the remaining 2 tablespoons lemon juice and stir to coat. Do this immediately to prevent the apple from browning.

3. Add the grapes, raisins, pecans, and celery to the apple. Stir to combine the ingredients.

4. Top the salad mixture with ½ cup of dressing, and stir gently until evenly mixed. If a more heavily dressed salad is desired, add more dressing at this point. You could also reserve some dressing to add to the salad after it has chilled.

5. The salad may be eaten immediately, but is best when chilled for about an hour. After chilling, add more dressing, if desired, and serve on a bed of greens. It may be kept, refrigerated, for 2 to 3 days.

Cauliflower "Egg" Salad

Servings: 8 half-cup servings

This is one of the most popular recipes from my blog, year after year. This plant-based spin on egg salad looks and tastes like the classic preparation and has a strikingly similar texture, thanks to steamed cauliflower. It makes a great sandwich or wrap. My favorite rendition is to serve it on top of a bowl of fresh greens. And talk about having a picnic-ready lunch—no worries about it spoiling!

Prep time: 35 minutes   **Cook time**: 20 minutes

1 medium head cauliflower

³/₄ cup raw cashews, soaked

1 teaspoon nutritional yeast flakes, to taste

¹/₄ cup unsweetened plant-based milk

2 generous tablespoons fresh lemon juice

¹/₂ teaspoon finely ground sea salt

dash black pepper

³/₄ teaspoon prepared mustard

¹/₄ teaspoon garlic salt

¹/₄ teaspoon granulated garlic

3 medium scallions, diced

¹/₃ medium red bell pepper, diced

1 medium stalk celery, diced

¹/₃ cup chopped green olives, diced

> **NOTES**
> – Soaking cashews is required prior to starting this recipe. See page 17 for quick-soak or overnight-soak instructions. That being said, the mayo can be made without soaking the cashews and will then yield a finished mayo with tiny unblended pieces of cashew that add a nice texture to the salad.

1. Chop the cauliflower into medium-size florets and steam in a countertop steamer or steamer basket in a pan on the stovetop for approximately 20 minutes or until fork-tender. Do not overcook; you do not want them to turn into mush when chopped. Immediately place the florets on a baking sheet to cool.

2. While the cauliflower is steaming, place the cashews in a blender with the nutritional yeast, plant-based milk, lemon juice, salt, pepper, mustard, garlic salt, and granulated garlic. If you chose not to soak the nuts prior to blending, blend on high speed until smooth or only small nut fragments remain (see note). The cashew mayo yields about ¾ cup. Set aside.

3. Place half of the cooled cauliflower florets into a food processor and pulse approximately 10 times into dice-size pieces. You may need to do this in batches if you're using a small food processor. Remove one batch from the processor before dicing the next. Alternatively, you could dice the cauliflower by hand. Continue until all florets have been diced. Pour the cauliflower into a large mixing bowl.

4. Add the diced scallions, peppers, celery, and olives to the cauliflower and gently mix. Lightly season the mixture with additional salt, black pepper, and garlic salt, if desired.

5. Pour the cashew mayo over the veggie mix and gently stir, being careful not to mash the cauliflower pieces. It is not necessary to use all of the cashew mayo to coat the diced veggies nicely and bring them together. If you prefer a wetter salad, add more mayo. Refrigerate the remaining mayo in a covered jar. Use within 5 to 7 days.

Variation

To make a nut-free version, replace the cashew mayo with ¾ cup vegan, nut-free, store-bought mayo. Reduce the nutritional yeast to ½ teaspoon, the plant-based milk to 2 tablespoons or until a saucy texture is achieved, and the lemon juice to 1 tablespoon. Then mix in the remaining seasonings from the cashew mayo recipe (see step 2).

Chickpea "Chicken" Salad

Guaranteed to satisfy your sandwich craving, this versatile salad offers an abundance of diverse tastes and textures in every bite! If you're feeling spicy, add some cayenne. Craving some garlic? Throw in a minced clove. Sweeten it by adding some grapes or dried cranberries—the list goes on and on! This salad is also tasty served wrapped in green leaf lettuce or a tortilla.

Prep time: 15 minutes   **Cook time:** none

¾ cup raw cashews, soaked

¼ cup unsweetened plant-based milk (I use cashew milk)

2 tablespoons fresh lemon juice

¾ teaspoon finely ground sea salt, divided

½ teaspoon granulated garlic, divided

¼ teaspoon prepared mustard, to taste

dash black pepper

1 (15-ounce) can chickpeas, rinsed and drained

1 medium stalk celery, diced

½ medium sweet onion, diced

3 medium radishes, diced, about ⅓ to ½ cup

> **NOTE**
> – Soaking cashews is required prior to starting this recipe. See page 17 for quick-soak or overnight-soak instructions.

1. Place the cashews in a food processor or blender. Add the milk and lemon juice. Blend until smooth, scraping the sides as needed. Add ½ teaspoon sea salt, ¼ teaspoon granulated garlic, the mustard, and black pepper and pulse a few times to mix.

2. Place the chickpeas in a food processor and pulse/chop until most chickpeas are about one-quarter to one-half their original size with a few whole ones remaining. Alternatively, you could chop the chickpeas by hand. Place the chopped chickpeas in a large mixing bowl.

3. Add the celery, onion, and radishes to the bowl with the chickpeas. Gently mix together with a wooden spoon. Sprinkle with the remaining ¼ teaspoon sea salt and ¼ teaspoon granulated garlic and mix again.

4. Pour the dressing over the mixture a few tablespoons at a time, mixing gently. Apply the dressing to taste, according to the level of creaminess you desire. This can be enjoyed immediately, but the flavors will blend exceptionally well if refrigerated. Serve on bread as a sandwich or on top of a bed of greens. Store leftovers in a sealed container in the refrigerator for up to 5 to 7 days.

Sweet and Spicy Corn and Bean Salad

Makes 8 cups

The multiple textures and flavors in this colorful salad make it a real palate pleaser. It's easy to prepare, too, and will look fantastic on your dinner table. Brimming with nutrients, it will satisfy your body—and it's a complete protein, to boot! Nutritionally speaking, this salad could be a one-stop shop for dinner. But since it has both sweet and spicy components, it would also be a great accompaniment in a large variety of meals.

Prep time: 20 minutes   **Cook time:** none

1 (15-ounce) can black beans

1 (15-ounce) can black-eyed peas

1 (15-ounce) can whole kernel sweet corn, unsweetened (or use fresh frozen)

$\frac{1}{2}$ large red bell pepper, diced, about $\frac{1}{2}$ cup rounded

$\frac{1}{2}$ large green bell pepper, diced, about $\frac{1}{2}$ cup rounded

$\frac{1}{2}$ cup diced celery

$\frac{1}{2}$ cup diced sweet onion

$\frac{1}{2}$ cup minced fresh parsley

2 tablespoons coconut nectar

2 tablespoons apple cider vinegar

$\frac{1}{4}$ cup avocado oil (walnut, grapeseed, or olive oil may be substituted)

$\frac{1}{8}$ teaspoon cayenne ground pepper (more if you prefer it spicier)

$\frac{1}{2}$ teaspoon, rounded, finely ground sea salt, to taste

> **NOTE**
> – Another perk of this salad is how easy it is to find the ingredients in the market during the colder months when a plentiful variety of fresh produce is not readily available.

1. Rinse and drain the black beans, black-eyed peas, and corn if not using frozen. Place them in a strainer and shake carefully to remove all excess moisture. Set aside to dry. Alternatively, spread beans, peas, and corn on a towel to absorb the extra moisture.

2. Place the diced red pepper, green pepper, celery, onion, and parsley in a large bowl. Set aside.

3. In a small bowl, whisk together the coconut nectar and apple cider vinegar. Then add the oil, cayenne pepper, and salt, one ingredient at a time, whisking after each addition.

4. Add the beans, peas, and corn to the large bowl with the chopped veggies and parsley. Stir gently to combine. Drizzle the dressing over the salad and mix thoroughly. Turn ingredients carefully to avoid mashing the beans and corn. Serve immediately or refrigerate for later. Store in an airtight container, and it will be delicious and crunchy on the second day as well! May be stored up to 4 to 5 days.

Baby Arugula and Corn Salad

Servings: 6

I'm not sure what I love most about this salad. It could be the way the bright yellow corn pops like little jewels against the garden green backdrop. Or how the peppery flavor of the arugula is complemented by the sweetness of the corn. Maybe it's because it only takes five minutes to prepare. Super-flexible and equally beautiful, it plates well in a bowl or on a platter and makes the perfect crisp salad to pair alongside creamy soup like the Quinoa Leek Bisque (page 50) or Thai Basil Alfredo (page 188).

Prep time: 5 minutes   **Cook time:** none

8 cups fresh baby arugula

1 tablespoon avocado oil

1 teaspoon lemon juice

¼ teaspoon garlic salt

sea salt and black pepper, to taste

1 cup whole kernel corn, drained (either fresh, canned, or frozen)

1. Place the arugula in a medium or large mixing bowl.

2. In a small bowl whisk together the avocado oil, lemon juice, garlic salt, and salt and black pepper for the dressing. This dressing can easily be doubled if a more heavily dressed salad is preferred.

3. Pour the dressing over the arugula and toss gently with tongs. Add the corn and gently toss again to incorporate. Serve immediately.

Creamy Avocado Cucumber Salad

Servings: 4

If you are an avocado lover, as I am, then you likely plan your meals around their ripeness. Lo and behold, this recipe came about from the presence of a ripe avocado and a significantly limited supply of other ingredients. Sometimes the best recipes come from asking questions like, "I wonder how avocado and cucumber taste together?" The answer: *incredible*. Since I created this recipe, I make it at least once a week, every week. It will definitely increase your salad diversity!

Prep time: 10 minutes   **Cook time**: none

2 ½ cups English cucumber sliced in ⅛-inch rounds, about 1 cucumber

½ medium red onion, sliced thin

1 large ripe avocado

2 tablespoons lime juice

2 tablespoons avocado oil

2 tablespoons unsweetened plant-based milk

¼ teaspoon finely ground sea salt, plus more for weeping the cucumber

⅛ teaspoon granulated garlic

⅛ teaspoon garlic salt

dash black pepper

> **NOTE**
> – For an oil-free version, replace the avocado oil in the recipe with water.

1. Place the sliced cucumber into a strainer and lightly coat with salt. Place in the sink for 5 minutes to allow excess water to weep from the cucumber. Rinse the cucumber, and blot it dry with a paper towel or a tea towel. Transfer the cucumber to a medium mixing bowl.

2. Add the red onion to the bowl with the cucumber and set aside.

3. *For the dressing:* Peel, quarter, remove the pit, and place the avocado in a food processor or blender. Lightly pulse to break the avocado into small pieces. Add the lime juice, avocado oil, plant-based milk, salt, granulated garlic, garlic salt, and black pepper. Blend until smooth. The dressing yields about ⅔ cup, depending on the size of the avocado.

4. Dress the cucumber and onion with the avocado mixture and lightly stir to coat. Serve immediately in a family-size dish or in individual servings.

Asparagus Quinoa Potato Salad

Servings: 12

This twist on traditional potato salad is packed with nutrients, tastes as wonderful as it looks, and is almost too pretty to eat! Bright purple potatoes and deep green asparagus make lovely additions to any table. Complemented by the nuttiness of quinoa and infusions of lemon and garlic, it will be impossible to stop at one serving. Serve warm or cold—it's delicious either way and picnic-friendly.

Prep time: 25 minutes   **Cook time:** 30 minutes

½ cup uncooked sprouted quinoa, rinsed and drained

1 cup filtered water

1 clove garlic, sliced

2 to 4 dashes sea salt, divided

1 pound fresh asparagus (thinner is better)

1 pound purple passion, two-bite potatoes, unpeeled

6 tablespoons lemon juice, from about 2 lemons

dash black pepper

2 teaspoons olive oil, divided

6 medium cloves garlic, minced and divided

1 cup raw cashews, soaked

½ shallot, peeled and sliced

½ cup unsweetened plant-based milk (I use cashew milk)

1. Place the quinoa in a strainer and rinse thoroughly in cold water. Place the quinoa, filtered water, sliced garlic, and a dash of salt in a saucepan and bring to a boil. Reduce the heat to a simmer and cook until the water is absorbed, about 8 minutes. The quinoa should appear translucent and the germ separates and wraps around the seed. Remove the pan from the heat to cool, and extract the garlic slices and discard them.

2. While the quinoa is cooking, wash the asparagus and potatoes, place on a tea towel, and blot dry. Cut off the thick, dry, bottom ends of the asparagus and cut the stalks into 1-inch lengths.

3. Cut the potatoes into small wedges and cover with water in a large saucepan. Add a dash of salt and bring the potatoes to a boil. Once boiling, reduce to a simmer and cook until the potatoes are fork-tender, about 8 to 10 minutes. I advise checking the potatoes at the 5-minute mark to ensure they are not cooking too fast, which will lead to them getting mushy and falling apart. Drain the

(continued on page 70)

NOTES

– Soaking cashews is required prior to starting this recipe. See page 17 for quick-soak or overnight-soak instructions.

– Quinoa can be made the night before and stored in an airtight container in the refrigerator. When you are ready to make the salad, remove the quinoa from the fridge. Allow it to come to room temperature while preparing the potato salad.

– For an oil-free version, replace the olive oil in the recipe with vegetable broth or water. See instructions for sautéing without oil on page 17.

potatoes and place them in a large bowl. Sprinkle with 3 tablespoons lemon juice and black pepper, toss to combine, and set aside allow to cool.

4. In a medium or large skillet, place 1 teaspoon oil and 3 minced garlic cloves in the center of the pan over medium heat. Spread the asparagus around the perimeter of the pan. Once the olive oil begins to bubble, combine the asparagus with the garlic and olive oil. Cook until the asparagus is somewhat tender but still retains some crunch, about 5 to 7 minutes. The garlic should be medium brown at this point. Spread the mixture onto a plate to cool. Do not place in a bowl or it will continue to cook and possibly weep. Reserve the oil and garlic in the pan for the salad dressing—no need to wash!

5. Place the remaining 1 teaspoon oil and the remaining 3 minced garlic cloves in a skillet. Sauté over low heat until the garlic is golden brown. Slowly add the remaining 3 tablespoons lemon juice to the garlic and olive oil while gently stirring to deglaze the pan. Caution: Pour the juice in a little at a time, as it may splatter. Remove from the heat and set aside to cool.

6. Place the soaked cashews in a food processor or a high-speed blender. Add the lemon garlic–olive oil mixture and shallot. Process until the nuts are broken down into small pieces. Add the plant-based milk and blend until the mixture has a thick dressing consistency. Add additional milk to thin if necessary, one tablespoon at a time.

7. Add the asparagus to the large bowl with the potatoes and gently mix. Once combined, add the quinoa and gently stir together. Pour half of the lemon-cashew dressing over the salad and lift and turn to gently combine, adding more dressing to taste. Season with sea salt and pepper and serve. This salad can be enjoyed at room temperature or chilled. If you are looking for a more robust flavor, the taste will intensify after refrigeration. Store it in an airtight container in the refrigerator for 5 to 7 days.

Tomato Vinaigrette

Makes about ³/₄ cup

Whether salads are your main meal or a side dish, an array of powerhouse dressings is a must. This vinaigrette is my staple dressing at home. It's wonderfully tangy and makes a great alternative to simple oil and vinegar. For the perfect application, be sure your lettuce is dry so the dressing clings to the leaves and does not end up at the bottom of the bowl.

Prep time: 5 minutes   **Cook time:** none

1 medium diced tomato, about ²/₃ cup

½ teaspoon finely ground sea salt

1 tablespoon olive oil

1 tablespoon red wine vinegar

dash cayenne pepper (more or less, to taste)

dash black pepper

Tip: Other ingredients, like cilantro or diced jalapeño, can be added for additional flavor.

> NOTE
> – This dressing can be made with or without the tomato skin. See step 1 to remove the tomato skin, if desired.

1. If you prefer to remove the tomato skin: Bring a small pot of water to a boil. Score the bottom of the tomato with an "X" through the layer of skin. Place the tomato in hot water for 1 minute. Remove it and place in an ice water bath until cool, about 2 minutes. Remove it from the cool water and peel. The skin should come off with little effort.

2. Place the diced tomato in a small bowl. Sprinkle the salt over the tomato and mash with a fork. Let the tomato sit for about 3 minutes while the salt extracts the juices from the tomato.

3. Add the remaining ingredients to the bowl with the tomato and tomato juice and whisk together. Taste and adjust the seasoning according to your preference. Store in an airtight container in the refrigerator for 3 to 4 days.

Cilantro Lime Vinaigrette

Makes ³/₄ cup

This wonderfully light and piquant vinaigrette is perfect for dressing delicate lettuces, like Bibb and mesclun. This dressing won't weigh down your leaves, keeping them light and airy while bringing an abundance of fresh flavor to your salad.

Prep time: 5 minutes   **Cook time:** none

¼ cup olive oil

¼ cup lime juice, from about 2 small limes

¼ packed cup diced fresh cilantro

⅓ cup plus 1 tablespoon unsweetened, mild-tasting plant-based milk (I use oat or cashew if nut-free is not necessary)

¼ to ½ teaspoon finely ground sea salt

dash black pepper, to taste

Place all the ingredients in a blender, adjusting salt and pepper to taste if needed. Pulse a few times, then blend on high speed until smooth. Store in an airtight container in the refrigerator for 3 to 4 days.

Ranch Dressing

Makes about 2 cups (depending on desired thickness)

This staple recipe can wear many hats. It makes a rich, plant-based, creamy salad dressing, but can easily convert to a spread for a sandwich or a dip for fresh veggies or crackers. I always have it on hand.

Prep time: 5 minutes, not including time to soak cashews   **Cook time:** none

1 cup raw cashews, soaked

²/₃ cup unsweetened plant-based milk or more if a thinner consistency is desired (I use cashew milk)

3 tablespoons lemon juice

1 teaspoon finely ground sea salt

³/₄ teaspoon prepared mustard

½ teaspoon granulated garlic

½ teaspoon onion powder

¼ teaspoon paprika

¼ teaspoon black pepper

1 tablespoon dried parsley

2 teaspoons dried chives

³/₄ to 1 teaspoon dried dill

NOTES

– Soaking cashews is required prior to starting this recipe. See page 17 for quick-soak or overnight-soak instructions.

For a reduced dill option: Alternatively, reduce dill by ½ teaspoon and add an additional ¼ teaspoon each of granulated garlic and onion powder.

---

1. Place the cashews plus the plant-based milk, lemon juice, salt, mustard, granulated garlic, onion powder, paprika, and black pepper in a blender and pulse to break down the cashews and combine the ingredients. Once the cashews are in very small pieces, turn the blender to high and blend until smooth, about 2 to 3 minutes, periodically pausing to scrape down the sides.

2. Add the parsley, chives, and dill, and blend until the herbs are small flecks. If you overblend, the dressing will turn a very light green from the herbs but will still taste delicious. Store in an airtight container in the refrigerator for 5 to 7 days.

CHAPTER 5

Toppers

Strawberry Peach Chia Jam

Makes about 2 cups

This recipe was born of necessity: My afternoon tea was lacking a sweet accompaniment—one without refined sugar—to make it complete. This jam became a regular teatime pairing, but its popularity in my house had me making double batches. It's the perfect spread for your morning toast or topping for your favorite pancake, and it has the ideal texture for the quintessential peanut butter and jelly sandwich. No pectin, gelatin, or canning required. And you can customize this recipe with your favorite fruits, like blueberries, raspberries, or pears.

Prep time: 5 minutes   **Cook time:** 20 minutes

1 cup chopped strawberries

1 cup sliced peach

2 tablespoons coconut nectar

1 tablespoon maple syrup

2 ½ teaspoons vanilla extract

1 ½ tablespoons chia seeds

1. Place the strawberries, peach, coconut nectar, maple syrup, and vanilla in a blender and combine until smooth.

2. Pour the mixture into a small saucepan and place over medium heat. Bring to a simmer, stirring occasionally, and reduce the heat to low for an additional 5 minutes.

3. Add the chia seeds and stir well. Simmer for an additional 15 minutes, stirring as necessary to prevent sticking and allow even cooking. Remove from the heat. The jam will continue to thicken after being removed from the heat.

4. Pour into a bowl and allow to cool. Store in the refrigerator in a sealed container for up to 2 weeks.

Easy Coconut Whipped Cream

Makes ³/₄ to 1 cup

Coconut has some naturally occurring sweetness, but if you like your whipped cream richer, you can add a sweetener, vanilla, or both. This topping has a very mild coconut flavor, almost imperceptible and makes it a great pairing with everything from a fruit cup to a piece of Fudgy Chocolate Cake (page 228). Just be sure to chill the coconut milk for at least 10–12 hours before you use it.

Prep time: 5 minutes   **Cook time:** none

1 (13.5-ounce) can classic coconut milk (do not use light)

1 to 2 tablespoons sweetener (optional; I recommend maple syrup or coconut nectar)

¹/₂ teaspoon vanilla extract or vanilla bean (optional)

NOTE

– To avoid possible issues, such as the coconut milk not separating or not hardening after refrigeration, gently shake the can before purchasing. If you hear liquid sloshing, you should avoid that one; it's a dud.

---

1. Chill a can of coconut milk in the refrigerator overnight. The coconut milk must be chilled for at least 10 to 12 hours for the cream and water to separate completely.

2. One hour before making the whipped cream, place a small or medium bowl (preferably metal) and beaters in the freezer to chill.

3. Carefully remove the can of coconut milk from the refrigerator so as not to mix the separated coconut cream and water. Flip it over so the bottom of the can is up. The coconut water will be at the top. Open the can and pour the coconut water off (I save it to use in smoothies). Scrape the remaining congealed cream into your chilled mixing bowl.

4. Beat the cream with an electric mixer until it appears smooth, about 30 seconds. Add the sweetener and vanilla and adjust to taste. Beat the cream again for 30 to 60 seconds, until blended and fluffy. Unlike a dairy-based version, coconut whipped cream will keep for 1 to 2 weeks in the refrigerator. It will be stiff when removed from the fridge, but it will soften as it warms.

Vegan Sour Cream

Makes 1 cup

Years ago I started using sour cream as a stand-in for mayonnaise to lighten recipes. Once I adopted a plant-based diet, I quickly needed a surefire replacement for my precious sour cream! This recipe has that precise thickness and tangy creaminess you need to bring a little richness to a dish or to cool off a hot enchilada or burrito. It also makes a great base for all types of dips such as Black Bean Dip (page 93).

Prep time: 5 minutes   **Cook time:** none

1 cup raw cashews, soaked

1/2 cup filtered water

2 tablespoons plus 1 teaspoon lemon juice

1 teaspoon apple cider vinegar

1/4 plus 1/8 teaspoon finely ground sea salt

1. Place all the ingredients in a high-speed blender. Blend on medium-low speed until the cashews are broken into small pieces, then blend on medium-high speed until smooth, periodically stopping to scrape the sides of the container.

2. Taste and adjust to preference. Add more salt or lemon juice for bite, or apple cider vinegar for tang, if desired. Refrigerate in an airtight container. This stays fresh for 1 week.

> **NOTES**
> – Soaking cashews is required prior to starting this recipe. See page 17 for quick-soak or overnight-soak instructions.

Vegan Ricotta Cheese

Makes 2 cups

One of the key components of lasagna, ricotta has that subtle texture and flavor that authenticates the entire dish. This recipe will convince even your most traditional cheese-loving friends and family that cooking with plant-based cheeses means sacrificing nothing. I always make a little extra to use as a spread on crackers for a late-afternoon snack!

This ricotta is delicious layered in the Vegan Zucchini Lasagna (page 181), on my Baked Ricotta Crostini (page 163), or spread on a cracker.

Prep time: 5 minutes   **Cook time**: none

2 cups raw cashews, soaked

3 tablespoons lemon juice
(juice of approximately 1 lemon)

1 1/2 teaspoons dried oregano

1 1/2 teaspoons finely ground
sea salt

1 teaspoon dried basil

1/4 teaspoon granulated garlic

pinch black pepper

1/2 cup cashew milk

> **NOTES**
> – Soaking cashews is required prior to starting this recipe. See page 17 for quick-soak or overnight-soak instructions.
>
> **Substitution:** Macadamia nuts or almonds may be substituted for cashews. Other mild-tasting plant-based milks may be substituted for cashew milk.

Place all the ingredients except the cashew milk in a food processor or high-speed blender. Blend until only small chunks remain, periodically pausing to scrape down the sides of the container. Add the cashew milk and blend until the desired texture for ricotta cheese is achieved. The traditional texture has the appearance of small curds. Store in a sealed container in the refrigerator for 5 to 7 days.

Vegan Parmesan Cheese

Makes 1 cup

When I was a kid, one of my favorite things was covering a slice of pizza with a layer of Parmesan cheese, shaken from one of those small glass jars with the metal lid. The soft, chewy clumps of buttery goodness gave that slice just what it needed. I refined this recipe over the course of weeks to perfect that distinctive taste and texture. The best part is it can be on your vegan pizza with just five ingredients and five minutes of preparation!

Prep time: 5 minutes **Cook time**: none

¾ cup raw cashews

1 teaspoon hemp seeds, raw and shelled, also known as hemp hearts

¾ teaspoon finely ground sea salt (more may be used if you prefer a saltier cheese)

¼ teaspoon granulated garlic

2½ teaspoons fresh lemon juice

1 teaspoon rice flour (optional)

1. Place the raw cashews and hemp seeds in a food processor and grind into very small pieces. Do not overgrind or you will end up with nut butter. The mixture should be coarse.

2. Add the salt, granulated garlic, and lemon juice, sprinkling evenly over the cashew mixture. Pulse a few times to mix the ingredients together. If you prefer a drier cheese, add the rice flour one-quarter teaspoon at a time, pulsing once or twice to blend, until desired texture is achieved. Store in an airtight container in the refrigerator for 1 week.

NOTES

– You can replace the hemp seeds with 1 teaspoon of olive oil, though this recipe would no longer be oil-free. The result is a small change in the flavor. The version with hemp seeds has earthy/grassy notes, while the version with olive oil enhances the tangy buttery notes. Using 1 teaspoon of olive oil does add a bit more moisture, so you may use about 2½ teaspoons of white rice flour to help granulate it a bit. If you find you don't care for the added tang, reduce the lemon juice by ½ teaspoon.

Rice flour: If you prefer a drier, more granulated Parmesan cheese, add rice flour ¼ teaspoon at a time until desired texture is achieved.

Blueberry Cream Cheese

Makes 2 cups

This fruity "cream cheese" recipe is incredibly flexible. I change it up depending on the time of year. The blueberry version is always on hand in my house, but it works equally well if you substitute a cup of chopped strawberries. When pomegranates are in season, I substitute the arils for blueberries. And the vibrant colors will look great on your breakfast table.

Prep time: 10 minutes **Cook time**: none

2 cups raw cashews, soaked

1 cup fresh blueberries

3 tablespoons fresh lemon juice

2 teaspoons apple cider vinegar

1 tablespoon coconut nectar or maple syrup

¼ teaspoon vanilla extract

⅛ teaspoon finely ground sea salt

> NOTE
> – Soaking cashews is required prior to starting this recipe. See page 17 for quick-soak or overnight-soak instructions. Since well-soaked cashews are the key to a smooth cream cheese, I use a double quick-soak method here if I use the hot water method of soaking. To do this, do the quick-soak method twice. The cashews are ready when they are soft and tender and not snappy when broken in half.

Place all the ingredients in a food processor in the order listed. A high-speed blender may be used if the motor is powerful and capable of blending very thick consistencies. Pulse a few times to break down the nuts, then blend until smooth, periodically pausing to scrape down the sides, about 3 to 5 minutes. The blueberry cream cheese can be served immediately, but flavors intensify after being refrigerated overnight. This keeps for several days if refrigerated in an airtight glass container.

Onion Chive Cream Cheese

Makes 2 cups

When that hot bagel pops out of the toaster, I am looking to put a healthy schmear on it before I take a bite. This Onion Chive "Cream Cheese" comes to the rescue every time: lush and creamy, with that tangy taste and rich texture I'm craving. If I want it extra bold, I dice up some green olives for topping and hit it with one good blast of cayenne. Equally great on a cracker or piece of toast, it also makes a fabulous dip with corn chips.

Prep time: 10 minutes   **Cook time:** none

2 cups raw cashews, soaked

3 tablespoons fresh lemon juice

2 teaspoons apple cider vinegar

3 teaspoons dried chives

2 teaspoons dehydrated onion

1 teaspoon finely ground sea salt

¼ teaspoon onion powder

⅛ teaspoon granulated garlic

⅓ cup unsweetened cashew milk, or substitute other unsweetened mild-tasting plant-based milk

> NOTE
> – Soaking cashews is required prior to starting this recipe. See page 17 for quick-soak or overnight-soak instructions. Since well-soaked cashews are the key to a smooth cream cheese, I use a double quick-soak method here if I use the hot water method of soaking. To do this, do the quick-soak method twice. The cashews are ready when they are soft and tender and not snappy when broken in half.

Place all the ingredients in a food processor in the order listed. A high-speed blender may be used if the motor is powerful and capable of blending very thick consistencies. Blend until smooth while periodically scraping down the sides, about 3 to 5 minutes. Onion Chive Cream Cheese can be served immediately, but flavors intensify after being refrigerated overnight. This keeps for several days if refrigerated in an airtight glass container.

Roasted Garlic and Red Pepper Spread

Makes 2 cups

Raw garlic can be intense and pungent. But once roasted, garlic transforms into a tempered, smooth, nutty deliciousness. Combine that roasted garlic with a little red bell pepper for some sweet tang and with cayenne pepper for a little zing. What a flavor pairing! The texture of this spread is incredibly creamy, rich, and smooth. Serve on fresh bread, crackers, fresh vegetables, or Easy Tortillas (page 103). It's so versatile; sometimes I will warm it in a pan with a little added cashew milk and make a pasta sauce.

Prep time: 10 minutes   **Cook time:** 35 minutes

1 1/4 cups raw cashews, soaked

1 bulb Roasted Garlic (page 19)

1/2 cup unsweetened cashew milk, or other mild-tasting unsweetened plant-based milk

1/4 large red bell pepper, membrane and seeds removed

1/2 teaspoon finely ground sea salt

1/4 teaspoon finely ground black pepper

1/8 teaspoon ground cayenne pepper

Place the soaked cashews in a high-speed blender. Squeeze about 8 of the roasted garlic cloves from their outer skin into the blender (more or fewer, depending on size and taste). Blend slowly at first, to allow the cashews to break down. Once the cashews are in small pieces, add the cashew milk, red bell pepper, salt, black pepper, and cayenne. Blend slowly at first, to keep seasonings from sticking to the sides of the container. Then blend on high speed until smooth and creamy. Taste the spread and adjust the salt, pepper, and cayenne to taste. If a thinner texture is desired, a small additional amount of milk can be added. This will keep well for 3 to 5 days if refrigerated in an airtight container.

NOTES

- Soaking cashews is required prior to starting this recipe. See page 17 for quick-soak or overnight-soak instructions.

- The only cooking required for this dish is roasting the garlic and heating the water used for the soaked cashews. The spread itself requires no cooking.

- To make this recipe oil-free, simply omit the oil when roasting the garlic.

Black-eyed Pea Hummus

Makes 1 1/2 cups

This is not your everyday hummus—it's a spin on the traditional recipe with a Cajun flair. The black-eyed peas lighten the recipe and the bell pepper brings a little sweetness to lift the flavor to a new level. Chile powder, paprika, and cumin make it pop with zestiness. This hummus can be served with crostini, crackers, and crudités, but I love it most with sautéed slices of yellow squash, zucchini, and red onion.

Prep time: 5 minutes **Cook time:** none

1 (15-ounce) can black-eyed peas, rinsed and drained

1/4 cup tahini

1/4 cup diced red, yellow, or orange bell pepper

3 tablespoons fresh lime juice, or 2 tablespoons lemon juice

1 large clove garlic, minced

3/4 teaspoon finely ground sea salt

3/4 teaspoon chile powder

1/2 teaspoon paprika

1/4 teaspoon cumin

2 to 5 dashes hot sauce, to taste

1 to 2 tablespoons warm water (optional)

1 teaspoon white vinegar, if using lime juice, to provide additional acidity

salt and black pepper, to taste

chopped chives, as garnish

> **NOTE**
> – I love the way lime juice works with these ingredients. It is a little sweeter than lemon juice and balances the earthy flavor of the black-eyed peas. I like to add a little white vinegar to bump up the acidity even more. Feel free to substitute lemon juice if you don't have any limes.

1. Place the black-eyed peas, tahini, bell pepper, lime or lemon juice, garlic, salt, chile powder, paprika, cumin, and hot sauce in a food processor. Pulse until the mixture is finely chopped, then blend until smooth, about 2 to 3 minutes.

2. If the hummus is too thick, drizzle the warm water through the chute of the food processor as it is running. Add one tablespoon at a time until the proper consistency is achieved. Taste the hummus and add the white vinegar if additional acidity is desired, and season with salt and pepper to taste. Transfer to a bowl or serving dish and garnish with the chives. Serve with crostini, crackers, or fresh vegetables. Store in an airtight container in the refrigerator for 3 to 4 days.

Black Bean Dip

Servings: 2 1/4 cups

If you want a party-pleaser that will have your guests asking for the recipe, serve this with a big bowl of blue corn tortillas. Unlike traditional black bean dips, where the bean itself is front and center, a blend of vegan sour cream, green chiles, and cilantro make this a creamy delight that matches up perfectly with your favorite corn chips. It will be the one bowl scraped clean at your table.

Prep time: 7 minutes (not including time to make the sour cream and refrigerate the dip)
Cook time: none

1 (15-ounce) can black beans, rinsed and drained

1/2 cup vegan mayo

1/2 cup Vegan Sour Cream (page 79), or store-bought

1 (4.5-ounce) can chopped green chilies, drained

2 tablespoons dried cilantro, or 1/4 cup fresh, diced

1 teaspoon chile powder

1/2 teaspoon garlic powder

2 to 3 dashes hot pepper sauce (optional)

> **NOTE**
> – If you are using Vegan Sour Cream (page 79) in this dip, advance prep is required to soak the cashews. In that case, this recipe is not nut-free. To prepare a nut-free dish, use store-bought, nut-free vegan sour cream.

Place the beans in a medium bowl and mash with a fork or potato masher. Stir in the mayo, sour cream, and chilies. Add the remaining ingredients and stir until all ingredients are combined. Cover and refrigerate for at least 1 hour. Serve with tortilla chips, crackers, or fresh vegetables. This will keep in an airtight container in the refrigerator for 3 to 5 days.

Garlic and Herb Dipping Oil

Makes 14 servings

This classic Italian-style dipping oil is perfect for swiping any bread of your choice to give it a little herbal love. Garlic, basil, and oregano bring the flavor, while the peppers add a nice pop. Store the dried blend in your spice cabinet and reach for it when a fresh loaf of bread or focaccia is cooling. A lovely jar of the seasoning blend, fresh loaf of bread, and bottle of gourmet olive oil make a great housewarming present!

Prep time: 5 minutes   **Cook time:** none

1 tablespoon dried basil

1 tablespoon dried oregano

1 tablespoon dried parsley

1 1/2 teaspoons dried crushed red pepper

1 1/2 teaspoons finely ground sea salt

1 teaspoon granulated garlic

1 teaspoon onion powder

several twists freshly cracked black pepper

extra-virgin olive oil, for serving

1. Combine all the dry seasoning ingredients in a small bowl, jar, or freezer bag. Mix well.

2. To store, place the herb mixture in an airtight container for 1 to 2 months. Make sure to shake the mixture of dried herbs prior to plating because the more finely ground herbs tend to sink to the bottom of the jar.

3. To serve, place the dry spice mixture on a shallow plate. Drizzle the desired amount of olive oil over the seasoning and stir together. Do not combine the dry seasoning blend with oil until ready to use. For individual servings, place 1 teaspoon dry seasoning blend on a small cocktail plate and cover with 1 tablespoon olive oil. More or less of both may be added, as desired. Discard any leftovers.

CHAPTER 6

Breads
and
Crackers

Brazilian "Cheese" Bread (Pão de Queijo)

Makes 20 mini rolls

Pão de Queijo translated literally means "bread of cheese." A traditionally gluten-free recipe from Brazil, these rolls are known for their light and airy texture. If you are unfamiliar with Brazilian Cheese Bread, you can expect a delicate crisp crust enveloping a chewy, soft, and glistening inside. So unique! This plant-based version tastes just like the original Brazilian recipe, "cheesy" goodness and all.

You can really have fun flavoring this bread. Sometimes I add a teaspoon of rosemary or Italian seasoning to the batter. An herbal olive oil, such as Garlic and Herb Dipping Oil (page 95), or zesty marinara also make tasty dipping sauces.

Prep time: 5 minutes   **Cook time:** 18 minutes

1 tablespoon golden flaxseed meal

3 tablespoons filtered water

1 cup tapioca flour or tapioca starch

½ cup potato starch (it is different from potato flour)

1 teaspoon finely ground sea salt

1 teaspoon baking powder

½ cup packed shredded vegan mozzarella cheese

⅔ cup unsweetened plant-based milk (I use cashew* for the mild, creamy flavor)

⅓ cup grapeseed, olive, or walnut* oil, plus more for greasing pan

*Use of these ingredients will no longer produce a nut-free version.

> **NOTE**
> – See my technique for measuring gluten-free flour (page 12) to ensure consistent measurements.

1. Preheat the oven to 400°F. Grease a mini muffin tin.

2. In a small bowl, stir together the golden flaxseed meal and filtered water. Set aside.

3. In a food processor or high-speed blender place the tapioca flour, potato starch, salt, and baking powder. Pulse 2 to 3 times to blend. Add the vegan cheese and pulse a few more times until the cheese is broken into very small pieces.

4. Stir the flax egg, then add it, the milk, and oil to the food processor or blender. Process well until smooth, about 30 seconds.

5. Pour or spoon the batter into mini muffin tin cups, filling to about one-eighth from the top. If any muffin cups remain empty, place 1 teaspoon of water in them. Bake for 18 to 20 minutes or until a toothpick inserted in the center comes out with only a few moist crumbs. The bread will be firm on the outside but puffy and lightly browned. The crust of the bread will be firm when first removed from the oven but will soften to a crisp after cooling for a minute or two. After taking the tin from the oven, remove the bread and place it on a cooling rack for 3 to 5 minutes and serve. Store the leftovers in an airtight container in the refrigerator for 3 to 5 days. The bread will reheat nicely in the microwave, wrapped in a damp paper towel, for 5 to 10 seconds for each roll or in the toaster oven for 1 to 2 minutes.

Rosmarino Flatbread

Makes 1 flatbread (9-inch diameter if baked as a circle)

Rosemary, garlic, and oregano balance pleasantly in this doughy and delicious—or crispy and crunchy—flatbread. Bake it to your desired texture! It makes a fabulous snack or lovely accompaniment to many meals. It's perfect for pairing alongside any number of Mediterranean dishes. Enjoy it fresh out of the oven with your favorite dipping oil or try my Garlic and Herb Dipping Oil (page 95).

Prep time: 12 minutes   **Cook time:** 25 minutes

½ cup tapioca starch or tapioca flour

½ cup arrowroot

½ cup white rice flour, plus a little extra for dusting the counter when kneading the dough

¼ cup sorghum flour or brown rice flour

¼ cup potato starch

2 teaspoons guar gum

1 tablespoon plus 2 teaspoons almond meal

2 ½ teaspoons baking powder

1 teaspoon finely ground sea salt

¼ teaspoon granulated garlic

½ teaspoon dried oregano

1 cup water

¼ cup olive oil, divided, plus more for greasing the baking sheet

2 large sprigs fresh rosemary (for topping)

coarsely ground sea salt (for topping, optional)

1. Preheat the oven to 375°F or 425°F (see note about baking options) and grease a baking sheet with olive oil.

2. In a medium bowl mix together the first seven ingredients. Add the baking powder, salt, granulated garlic, and dried oregano. Mix together well, making sure to evenly distribute the baking powder.

3. In a separate small bowl combine the water and 2 tablespoons olive oil. Add this to the dry ingredients and mix well with a wooden spoon until combined. There should be no dry, powdery ingredients remaining. If there are, add water 1 tablespoon at a time and mix until all of the ingredients are in small clumps. The dough should form into a ball with ease but not be wet.

4. Place a small handful of white rice flour on your work surface and spread it out. Place the dough on the floured surface. Knead 4 or 5 times. Form the dough into a ball and place on a greased baking sheet. With oiled fingers, spread the dough into a circle or rectangle about ½ inch thick. Make small circular dimples with your fingertips over the surface of the

NOTES

– Cooking time and temperature vary depending on desired texture. For a crispy crust and a soft inside, bake at 375°F for 20 minutes then increase temperature to 425°F for an additional 5 minutes. For a crispy golden brown crust and a crunchier inside, bake at 425°F for 35 minutes or until golden brown.

– See my technique for measuring gluten-free flour (page 12) to ensure consistent measurements.

dough. Brush the top and sides of the dough with the remaining olive oil.

5. Dice 1 tablespoon of fresh rosemary and sprinkle on the dough. Cut whole leaves or small sprigs and place them in the center. If desired, sprinkle with coarse sea salt.

6. Follow the instructions in the Notes about baking to the desired texture. When the baking is complete, remove from the oven and place on a cooling rack. Cut with a knife or pizza cutter and serve.

Easy Tortillas

Makes 10 six-inch tortillas

When you're hankering for a dish that is heavy on the filling and light on the delivery device, nothing works better than a tortilla. These gluten-free tortillas have great taste and texture and require only four main ingredients. Sandwich some vegan cheese and veggies between two for a fabulous plant-based quesadilla. They can also be used to make a pan of enchiladas, a batch of tacos, or your favorite wrap.

Prep time: 10 minutes   **Cook time:** 40 minutes

1 tablespoon golden flaxseed meal

3 tablespoons warm water

1 1/2 cups white rice flour, plus more for flouring your surface when rolling the tortillas

1/2 cup arrowroot

1/2 teaspoon finely ground sea salt

3/4 cup boiling water

> NOTES
> - Although this recipe is oil-free, I like to lightly rub oil on the pan when I cook the tortillas to give them a little extra flexibility.
>
> - Prepared dough can be wrapped in plastic wrap and refrigerated for 3 to 5 days. This way, you can make the dough ahead of time and use it on an as-needed basis for pan-fresh tortillas!
>
> - See my technique for measuring gluten-free flour (page 12) to ensure consistent measurements.

1. In a small bowl combine the golden flaxseed meal and warm water and set aside.

2. In a medium-size mixing bowl combine the white rice flour, arrowroot, and salt.

3. Add the flax mixture to the flour mixture and stir together. A slicing motion with a wooden spoon combines the two thoroughly. Then add the boiling water and mix together with a wooden spoon. Once most of the dry ingredients are incorporated, form the dough into a ball. The dough should stick together with

Helpful hint: Don't overpay for arrowroot! In most cases, it's not economical to buy arrowroot in the spice section of your grocery store. It is usually much cheaper when purchased in a larger quantity.

ease but not be wet. If the dough is too dry add more hot water 1 tablespoon at a time. If too moist add more rice flour 1 tablespoon at a time.

4. Coat the work surface with white rice flour and knead the dough 4 to 6 times. Keep the dough wrapped in plastic wrap or a tea towel to prevent the exterior from drying out while making the tortillas.

5. To make the tortillas, flour the surface as needed with white rice flour. Break off a portion of the dough and form it into a ball (using 2 tablespoons of dough for each will yield about 10 6-inch tortillas). Press each dough ball into the flour on the surface and flatten two times on each side, then roll out with a rolling pin or continue pressing with your hands until 6 inches wide.

6. Cook the tortilla in a medium nonstick skillet over medium or medium-high heat for about 2 minutes on each side. I like to lightly grease my pan with olive oil to make the tortillas more pliable. Place the finished tortillas on a baking sheet or plate lined with parchment paper to cool. Leftover tortillas can be refrigerated in a sealed bag for a few days. To reheat, cover with wax paper or a damp paper towel and microwave on high for 15 seconds.

VEGAN QUESADILLA

To make a plant-based quesadilla, I prefer a mix of shredded vegan cheddar and mozzarella (about ¼ cup total) and fresh chopped jalapeño and onion, but any combination of veggies would be delicious! Sprinkle desired filling (but not too thick, or the cheese won't melt) on one tortilla and top with a second tortilla. Place in a nonstick pan over medium-low heat until the cheese begins to melt, about 3 to 5 minutes. Then flip to the opposite side and complete melting.

Sandwich Bread

Servings: 16 half-inch slices

Every day more new off-the-shelf options for gluten-free bread appear. But most are not plant-based or refined sugar-free. Not only does this loaf hit all of those markers, it is also nut-free and it doesn't require any kneading. Moist and chewy, this bread is substantial enough to support heavy ingredients, plus it can be sliced thin without falling apart. Perfect for toast with jam in the morning, a sandwich for lunch, or for a fabulous panini at dinner!

Prep time: 15 minutes   **Cook time:** 35 to 40 minutes

1 cup unsweetened plant-based milk at room temperature

5 tablespoons golden flaxseed meal

¾ cup warm water, about 110°F

2 tablespoons maple syrup or coconut nectar

1 packet or 2 ¼ teaspoons active dry yeast

¾ cup tapioca flour or starch

¾ cup white rice flour

½ cup gluten-free oat flour

½ cup potato starch

½ cup arrowroot

2 teaspoons baking powder

¾ teaspoon baking soda

½ teaspoon finely ground sea salt

3 tablespoons refined coconut oil, melted

2 teaspoons apple cider vinegar or lemon juice

> **NOTE**
> – See my technique for measuring gluten-free flour (page 12) to ensure consistent measurements.

1. Preheat the oven to 350°F. Make sure the oven rack is in the center of the oven.

2. In a small bowl, combine the plant-based milk and golden flaxseed meal. Set aside for at least five minutes until thickened and slightly gelled.

3. Pour ¾ cup warm water into a small mixing bowl. It should be slightly warmer than skin temperature, about 110°F. It is important not to make the water too hot or it will kill the yeast. Stir the maple syrup into the water and sprinkle the yeast on top. Then gently stir and set aside to proof for at least 5 minutes. You will see a foamy layer develop as the yeast multiplies.

4. While the yeast and flax mixtures are developing, combine the tapioca flour, white rice flour, oat flour,

potato starch, arrowroot, baking powder, baking soda, and salt in a large mixing bowl and stir well. I like to use a whisk to ensure that everything is thoroughly combined.

5. Add the coconut oil and apple cider vinegar to the flax mixture and stir until combined. Using a small whisk is helpful for this step. Then add the flax mixture to the yeast mixture and stir gently to combine.

6. Add the wet ingredients to the dry ingredients and stir gently with a wooden spoon until combined. Be sure to not overmix, or you will end up with a flatter loaf. The consistency should be more like batter than dough.

7. Pour into a greased 8½ x 4½-inch loaf pan (or a 9 x 5-inch loaf pan, which will yield a shorter loaf). Set aside in a warm area to proof for about 8 to10 minutes. The amount the loaf rises will depend on many variables in your environment, such as room temperature and age of the yeast used. Do not allow the loaf to rise higher than half an inch from the top of the pan or it may overflow when baking; this is normal with gluten-free breads as they lack structure.

8. Place the loaf pan in the center of the oven and bake about 35 to 40 minutes or until a toothpick inserted deep into the center comes out clean. Remove the pan from the oven and place on a baking rack to cool, about 30 minutes. Once the loaf is cool enough to handle with bare hands, run a butter knife around the edges of the pan and invert to remove the loaf. It should come out with relative ease. To store, I wrap the loaf in wax paper and place in an airtight container in the refrigerator. It will keep for about 1 week.

Graham Crackers

Servings: 40 crackers

Perfect for a quick snack or to use as a graham cracker crust, this recipe can be whipped up in no time. Crispy and with a hint of molasses, these will hit the spot with a cup of tea. Better yet, put a dollop of vegan ice cream between two of the crackers after they've cooled.

Prep time: 15 minutes   **Cook time:** 22 minutes

3 tablespoons unsweetened plant-based milk (more may be used when combining dough)

1 tablespoon golden flaxseed meal

1 cup gluten-free oat flour

1 cup white rice flour

½ cup tapioca flour or tapioca starch

3 tablespoons coconut sugar

½ teaspoon baking soda

¼ teaspoon finely ground sea salt

3 tablespoons coconut oil, melted

3 tablespoons mashed very ripe banana (about half a medium banana)

2 tablespoons blackstrap molasses

2 teaspoons vanilla extract

coconut sugar (optional)

cinnamon (optional)

> NOTE
> – See my technique for measuring gluten-free flour (page 12) to ensure consistent measurements.

1. Preheat the oven to 350°F. Cut 2 sheets of parchment paper to line 2 baking sheets and a third sheet of parchment the same size. Set aside.

2. In a small mixing bowl, stir together the plant-based milk and golden flaxseed meal and set aside.

3. In a medium mixing bowl, combine the oat flour, white rice flour, tapioca flour, coconut sugar, baking soda, and salt and mix thoroughly.

4. Add the oil, banana, molasses, and vanilla to the milk and flax and stir or whisk to mix well.

5. Add the wet ingredients to the dry ingredients and stir well. Once the dough begins to form, you will need to complete the mixing with your hands. Fold and press the dough until thoroughly combined. If the dough is too dry and not binding together, an additional tablespoon of plant-based milk may be added. Form the dough into a ball and cut it in half.

6. Form one half into a ball. Place it between two of the three sheets of parchment paper. Flatten the dough with your palm to about 1 to 1½ inches thick. Use a rolling pin to roll it into a rectangle about ⅛ inch thick. If there are some thick areas, you can press them with your palm.

7. Leaving the dough on the bottom sheet of parchment paper, remove the top sheet and transfer the dough to the baking sheet. Using a pizza cutter or sharp knife cut dough into 1 to 2 inch squares. Do not separate the squares prior to baking. Then use a fork to poke holes in the top of the crackers. For a cinnamon graham, sprinkle with the coconut sugar and cinnamon. Bake 22 to 25 minutes until crisp. Remove from the oven and allow to cool on a baking sheet. Repeat steps 6 and 7 on the second half of the dough, reusing the top sheet of parchment paper. Graham crackers will keep in an airtight container at room temperature for a minimum of 1 week.

Tip: Unlike refined sugar, which has zero nutritional value, blackstrap molasses contains vital vitamins and minerals, such as iron, calcium, magnesium, vitamin B6, and selenium.

NOTES

- The cooking time is to par-bake the crust. This is necessary prior to making your pizza.

- See my technique for measuring gluten-free flour (page 12) to ensure consistent measurements.

Gluten-Free Pizza Crust

Makes 2 twelve-inch pizza crusts or 1 sixteen-inch pizza crust

What is the hardest sell in getting folks to try plant-based and gluten-free food? Pizza. No one wants to give up pizza, or they're certain that a gluten-free, plant-based crust can't come close to their favorite pie. This recipe may have had the most renditions as I developed it and until I considered it to be just right. The biggest hurdle: droop. I wanted the crust to have that classic New York style droop when you picked up a slice. I was determined to make a gluten-free and plant-based pizza crust that didn't have a crunchy or crumbly texture and didn't taste like, well, cardboard. It was so worth the time. Finally, a doughy, chewy crust that tastes perfect with your favorite toppings. It even makes a great white pizza!

Prep time: 18 minutes   **Cook time**: 7 minutes (to par-bake crust)

1 cup warm water

2 tablespoons maple syrup or coconut nectar at room temperature

1 packet or 2 ¼ teaspoons active dry yeast

1 cup tapioca flour or tapioca starch

1 cup white rice flour

½ cup brown rice flour

½ cup arrowroot

1 teaspoon finely ground sea salt

2 tablespoons olive oil or melted coconut oil, plus more for greasing the pan

1. Preheat the oven to 425°F. Grease the pizza pan(s) with olive oil.

2. Pour the warm water into a small mixing bowl. It should be slightly warmer than skin temperature, about 110°F. It is important not to make the water too hot or it will kill the yeast. Stir the maple syrup into the water and sprinkle the yeast on top. Gently stir and set aside to proof for at least 5 minutes. You will see a foamy layer develop as the yeast multiplies.

3. While the yeast is proofing, combine the tapioca flour, white rice flour, brown rice flour, and arrowroot in a medium mixing bowl and set aside.

4. Once the yeast mixture has proofed, add the salt and oil and stir to blend. Then add the wet ingredients to the dry ingredients and stir with a wooden spoon until combined. Once the dough begins to form, you will need to complete the mixing with your hands. Fold and press the dough until thoroughly combined. If the

dough is too dry and not binding together, add an additional tablespoon of plant-based milk. Once combined, knead the dough in the bowl by first pressing the dough ball with the heel of your palm to flatten it. Fold the dough in half over itself. Turn the dough one-quarter turn and repeat the process. Do this about 4 to 6 times. Form the dough into a ball and place it in a bowl. Cover the bowl with a tea towel and let the dough rest for 5 minutes.

5. The dough makes one 16-inch pizza or may be split in half for two 12-inch pizzas. Place the dough ball in the center of a greased pizza pan. Press the dough to flatten it and cover it with a piece of plastic wrap large enough to cover the entire pan. Using the palm of your hand or a rolling pin, press or roll the dough to fit the size of the pan, rotating the pan when necessary. Crimp the edges with your fingers to form a crust. Remove the plastic wrap. The dough should be about ⅜ inch thick for the 16-inch pizza and ¼ inch thick for the 12-inch pizzas.

6. Pre-bake the plain crust for about 7 minutes.

To make a pizza

Remove the crust from the oven and add sauce, vegan cheese, and toppings of choice. Return to the oven and bake for additional 10 minutes or until the crust is beginning to brown.

Basil Crackers

Servings: About 40 one- to two-inch crackers

These crackers' subtle herbal notes pair well with your favorite bottle of wine. I like to serve them with fresh fruit and plant-based cheeses for a healthy version of a charcuterie board.

Prep time: 15 minutes   **Cook time:** 20 to 30 minutes

2 tablespoons golden flaxseed meal

1/3 cup unsweetened cashew milk or mild-tasting plant-based milk

3 cups almond meal

1/2 cup chopped fresh basil

1/2 teaspoon baking soda

1/4 teaspoon sea salt

3 tablespoons unsweetened applesauce

2 tablespoons walnut oil or grapeseed oil

2 teaspoons apple cider vinegar

sea salt, garlic salt, or cayenne pepper, for topping (optional, use any combination desired)

> **NOTE**
> – See my technique for measuring gluten-free flour (page 12) to ensure consistent measurements.

1. Preheat the oven to 325°F. Cut three pieces of parchment paper to fit a large baking sheet.

2. In a small bowl, whisk together the golden flaxseed meal and plant-based milk. Set aside.

3. In a medium or large mixing bowl, stir together the almond meal, basil, baking soda, and salt.

4. Add the applesauce, oil, and vinegar to the flax mixture and whisk well. Add the wet ingredients to the dry ingredients and stir well. Once the dough begins to form, you will need to complete the mixing with your hands. Lifting and folding until ingredients are completely combined (like kneading pizza dough, step 4, page 112) works well. Form the dough into a ball and cut into two halves.

5. Form one half into a ball. Place between two of the three sheets of parchment paper and flatten with your hands to about 1 inch thick. Using a rolling pin, roll

to about ⅛ inch thick. Try to roll into a rectangle. By limiting edges within the parchment paper, the dough will fit on a baking sheet. If needed, press thicker areas with your hands.

6. Remove the top sheet of parchment paper and transfer the bottom sheet with the rolled dough onto the baking sheet. Score the dough into 1- to 2-inch squares with a pizza cutter or a sharp knife. Sprinkle salt or desired seasoning on top of the dough. Bake for approximately 30 minutes, or until the desired level of crispiness is achieved. Let the crackers cool on the baking sheet for at least 20 minutes, then break them apart on scored lines. Repeat steps 5 and 6 for the second half of the dough, reusing the top sheet of parchment paper. Store in an airtight container. This will keep for several days.

Variation

For thicker and softer crackers that resemble flatbread, roll the dough a little bit thicker—by about one-quarter inch. Follow the remaining steps in the recipe.

Homestyle Buttermilk Biscuits

Servings: 12

I love these homestyle biscuits. Of course, they don't contain butter or milk—they should really be titled *Better*milk Biscuits! They make a terrific side and are the perfect size for cucumber sandwiches. Or pair them with my Eggless Chickpea Scramble (page 28) and Portobello Bacon (page 30) for a hearty breakfast that will start your day right.

Prep time: 20 minutes   **Cook time:** 18 minutes

1 tablespoon distilled white vinegar

1 cup unsweetened, mild-tasting plant-based milk such as oat milk

2 tablespoons vegan butter, chilled

2 tablespoons refined coconut oil, chilled

1 cup white rice flour

1 cup potato starch (not potato flour)

1 tablespoon arrowroot

4 teaspoons baking powder

3/4 teaspoon finely ground sea salt

1/4 teaspoon baking soda

1. Place the vinegar in a 1-cup measuring cup and fill the remainder of the cup with the plant-based milk to create buttermilk. Whisk together and refrigerate for at least 10 minutes. In a small bowl place the vegan butter and coconut oil and refrigerate as well.

2. In a medium or large mixing bowl, add the remaining ingredients. Stir with a wooden spoon to combine.

3. Add the vegan butter and coconut oil in small, grape-size pieces to the dry ingredients. Use a pastry blender or two bread knives cutting in opposite directions to blend the dry ingredients with the butter and oil. Only small pea-size pieces of butter or oil should remain. Do this at a swift pace to prevent the butter and solid coconut oil from melting. Place the bowl in the refrigerator or freezer for 5 minutes.

4. Remove the flour mixture from the refrigerator or freezer and make a well in the center of the mix. Add

---

NOTE

– See my technique for measuring gluten-free flour (page 12) to ensure consistent measurements.

the chilled buttermilk. Mix together with a wooden spoon only until the buttermilk is just incorporated (do not overmix) and no liquid is visible. The dough will appear sticky and wet.

5. Preheat the oven to 450°F. Line a baking sheet with parchment paper.

6. Flour your work surface lightly with potato starch. Place the dough on the floured surface and form a ball. Press down until 1 to 2 inches thick and lightly flour the top side of the dough. Fold the dough in half on top of itself, press, and rotate one-quarter turn. Press together the dough, if still wet and not yet sticking together, and lightly flour the top side again. Fold the dough over on top of itself again and turn, repeating all steps 5 to 6 times until the dough is no longer very wet and holds its form. Remember, less is more when mixing, kneading, and forming the dough. Overworking the dough will make it rigid, and this will prevent it from rising during baking.

7. Press the dough into a 1-inch-thick circle. Cut the biscuits with a 2-inch biscuit or cookie cutter. Press straight down and twist to make a clean cut. Place the cut biscuit on the baking sheet. Biscuits should be placed very close together, not touching, but not more than ¾ inch apart. Repeat until all biscuits have been cut by reforming scraps of dough into a ball and pressing again into a 1-inch round. Try to handle the dough as little as possible to keep them lighter. The biscuits from the dough that has been handled more will have a denser texture.

8. Bake for 15 to 20 minutes. The biscuits should rise during baking and become very light golden brown on top. Remove from the oven and transfer to a cooling rack. Serve immediately. The biscuits will have a crisp outside and soft, airy inside.

Zucchini Bread

Servings: 16

This bread makes me look forward to autumn. When zucchinis become plentiful, I make loaves of this bread weekly. It's moist, chewy, and delicious, and there is virtually no time of day that doesn't beg for a little slice. It also makes a great pairing to serve alongside appetizers or with a heavy meal. The spices provide a nice palate cleanser while not overwhelming other dishes. And if a wine tasting is part of your evening, this bread's scents and tastes match equally well with a selection of reds or whites. If a more aromatic version is desired, ¼ teaspoon of ground ginger could be added for a pop.

Prep time: 15 minutes   **Cook time:** 30 to 35 minutes

2 cups grated zucchini, about 1 medium zucchini

2 tablespoons golden flaxseed meal

¹⁄₂ cup unsweetened plant-based milk

1 cup gluten free oat flour

¹⁄₂ cup sweet white sorghum flour

¹⁄₂ cup almond meal

²⁄₃ cup coconut sugar

¹⁄₄ cup arrowroot

2 teaspoons baking powder

1¹⁄₂ to 2 teaspoons cinnamon (use more if you like cinnamon)

³⁄₄ teaspoon finely ground sea salt

¹⁄₄ teaspoon finely ground nutmeg

¹⁄₂ cup unsweetened applesauce (or sweetened, if a sweeter bread is desired)

(continued on the following page)

1. Preheat the oven to 350°F. Lightly grease (with walnut, grapeseed, or avocado oil) or line an 8 x 8-inch pan with parchment paper. Line the bottom of a bowl with a paper towel to soak up any extra moisture and place the grated zucchini in the bowl. Set aside.

2. In a small bowl, whisk together the golden flaxseed meal and plant-based milk. Set aside.

3. In a medium or large mixing bowl, stir together the flours, almond meal, coconut sugar, arrowroot, baking powder, cinnamon, salt, and nutmeg until thoroughly combined.

4. Add the applesauce, raisins, and vanilla to the flax mixture and whisk to combine. Then add the wet ingredients to the dry ingredients and combine well with a wooden spoon. This may take a minute or two as the batter is very dense.

5. If your grated zucchini shreds are much longer than about ½ inch, place them in a pile on a cutting board

½ cup raisins, chopped (I like to use golden raisins)

1½ teaspoons vanilla extract

NOTES

- See my technique for measuring gluten-free flour (page 12) to ensure consistent measurements.

- To make this bread nut-free, replace the almond meal with an equal amount of tapioca flour.

and chop the pile once or twice. Gently stir the zucchini into the batter. If the batter is too thick to combine, add 1 to 2 tablespoons of additional plant-based milk. Pour the batter into the pan and use a spatula to spread it evenly. Bake for 30 to 35 minutes, until a toothpick inserted comes out clean. Remove from the oven and place on a cooling rack. Once cool, the bread may be cut and then removed from the pan. The bread will keep nicely in an airtight container at room temperature for a day or two. After that I recommend storing it in the refrigerator.

Blueberry Banana Bread

Makes 12 slices

The best of both worlds: a rich blueberry muffin and moist banana bread. This recipe started as a *what if* and ended up the dessert bread most requested for the holiday table. It is delicious when fresh baked, or a toasted thick slice with a schmear of my Coconut Butter/Manna (page 21) is a great evening treat.

Prep time: 10 minutes   **Cook time:** 48 minutes

³/₄ cup applesauce

¹/₂ cup mashed very ripe banana (approximately 1 medium banana)

3 tablespoons unsweetened plant-based milk, such as oat milk

3 tablespoons golden flaxseed meal

1 tablespoon fresh lemon juice

2 teaspoons vanilla extract

1 cup gluten free oat flour

¹/₂ cup tapioca flour or starch

¹/₂ cup white rice flour

¹/₂ cup potato starch (not potato flour)

¹/₂ cup coconut sugar

1 teaspoon baking soda

¹/₂ teaspoon baking powder

¹/₂ teaspoon finely ground sea salt

1 ¹/₂ cups fresh blueberries

> **NOTES**
> – For a sweeter bread, double the amount of plant-based milk and add an extra ¼ cup of coconut sugar.
>
> – See my technique for measuring gluten-free flour (page 12) to ensure consistent measurements.

1. Preheat the oven to 350°F and grease (with walnut, grapeseed, or avocado oil) an 8½ x 4½ x 2½-inch loaf pan or line with parchment paper.

2. In a small bowl, whisk together the applesauce, banana, plant-based milk, flaxseed meal, lemon juice, and vanilla. Set aside.

3. In a medium or large mixing bowl, stir together the flours, potato starch, coconut sugar, baking soda, baking powder, and salt.

4. Add the wet ingredients to the dry ingredients and mix together with a wooden spoon. Gently fold in the blueberries, being careful not to mash them.

5. Pour the batter into the loaf pan. Bake for 45 minutes, until a toothpick inserted in the center comes out clean when removed. Remove from the oven and cool in the loaf pan for 30 minutes. Gently loosen the sides with a bread knife. Remove from the pan and place the loaf on a rack to cool completely. Store in an airtight container in the refrigerator for 5 to 7 days.

CHAPTER 7

Nibbles
and
Snacks

Alpha Omega Granola

Makes 16 half-cup servings

Alpha and Omega are the first and last letters of the Greek alphabet—the beginning and end. Just like this granola—vitamins, minerals, fiber, complex carbohydrates, plant-based protein, and omega-3s—the beginning to end of the macro and micronutrients! And as it is nut-free, it's safe for those with nut sensitivities too. It's never been so easy to make a recipe that is a breakfast, snack, and dessert all rolled into one. Serve it in a bowl with your favorite plant-based milk or take it on the go for a snack that fuels you for the rest of your day.

Prep time: 15 minutes   **Cook time**: 45 minutes

2 cups gluten-free rolled oats

½ cup buckwheat groats

½ cup sprouted pumpkin seeds

½ cup unsweetened coconut flakes

¼ cup raw hemp seed, shelled

¼ cup chia seeds

¼ cup golden flaxseed meal

⅓ cup dried cherries

⅓ cup golden raisins

⅓ cup dried apricots

¼ cup coconut oil

¼ cup maple syrup or coconut nectar

2 tablespoons coconut sugar

1 teaspoon cinnamon

¼ teaspoon finely ground sea salt

1 teaspoon vanilla extract

> **NOTES**
> Here's the nutritional breakdown:
>
> **Omega-3s:** raw shelled hemp seed, chia seeds, and golden flaxseed meal.
>
> **Plant-based protein:** gluten-free rolled oats, buckwheat groats, sprouted pumpkin seeds, raw shelled hemp seeds, chia seeds, golden flaxseed meal, and unsweetened coconut flakes.
>
> **Antioxidants:** gluten-free rolled oats, buckwheat groats, sprouted pumpkin seeds, raw shelled hemp seeds, chia seeds, golden flaxseed meal, unsweetened coconut flakes, dried cherries, raisins, apricots, cinnamon, coconut oil, maple syrup, and coconut sugar.

1. Preheat the oven to 275°F.

2. Add the first seven ingredients to a medium-size mixing bowl and stir together with a wooden spoon. Place the cherries, raisins, and apricots on a cutting board and chop into small pieces. Add the dried fruit to the mixture in the bowl and stir together until combined. Set aside.

3. In a small saucepan combine the coconut oil, maple syrup, coconut sugar, cinnamon, and salt. Whisk together over medium heat until the coconut sugar is melted. Remove from the heat and stir in the vanilla. Pour the syrup over the dry mixture in the bowl and mix with a wooden spoon until thoroughly combined.

4. Spread the mixture on a parchment-lined baking sheet evenly with a wooden spoon or spatula. Bake for 45 minutes or until light brown and crunchy. Remove from the oven and allow to cool for 1 hour before breaking apart into pieces. Store in a zip-top bag at room temperature for 1 week or in a zip-top bag in the refrigerator up to 2 weeks.

Tip: This recipe can be customized with different dried fruits or nuts.

Healthier Candied Pecans

Makes 1 cup

SF

A five-minute prep, let your oven do the rest! This one has been a perennial favorite recipe on my blog, especially during the holiday months. Cinnamon and vanilla marry perfectly with fresh roasted nuts that have a delightful candied shell. The recipe is flexible enough that you can also use almonds, walnuts, or a combination of your choosing.

Prep time: 5 minutes   **Cook time**: 30 minutes

1 tablespoon golden flaxseed meal

1 tablespoon coconut nectar

1 tablespoon vegan butter or coconut oil, melted

1 tablespoon nut milk (I use cashew)

1 ½ teaspoons vanilla extract

1 rounded cup raw pecans

¼ to ½ teaspoon cinnamon, to taste

3 tablespoons coconut sugar, divided

1. Preheat the oven to 275°F.

2. In a small mixing bowl combine the flaxseed meal, coconut nectar, vegan butter, nut milk, and vanilla. Stir well. Let stand 1 minute or more.

3. Mix the pecans into the flax mixture. Stir well and let stand while preparing the cinnamon sugar and baking sheet.

4. In a zip-top bag, spoon in the cinnamon and two tablespoons of coconut sugar. Close the bag and shake it to mix well. Place parchment paper on a baking sheet.

5. Using a slotted spoon, transfer the nuts from the bowl with the flax mixture to the bag with the cinnamon-sugar mixture. The nuts should be generously coated with flax mixture. Close the bag and shake well to cover them with cinnamon and sugar.

6. Pour the nuts onto the baking sheet and spread them evenly in a single layer. Sprinkle the remaining tablespoon of coconut sugar over the nuts. Bake for about 30 minutes. Remove from the oven and allow the nuts to cool on the baking sheet before removing. Store the nuts in an airtight container at room temperature for 1 week.

Roasted Chipotle Chickpeas

Makes 7 quarter-cup servings

I am always on the lookout for healthy snack foods that satisfy a savory craving while giving my body nourishment. Chickpeas, an impressive source of plant-based protein and many other nutrients, do just that. This recipe requires only 5 minutes of active prep time and just a few ingredients. Plus you can customize it to your personal taste! Desire more spice? Add more ground chipotle or substitute a different heat source like chile powder. Want something milder? Just add sea salt. You will be reaching for them before that temptress, potato chips!

Prep time: 5 minutes   **Cook time**: 40 minutes

1 (15-ounce) can chickpeas

1 tablespoon olive oil

½ teaspoon finely ground sea salt, to taste

½ teaspoon ground chipotle chile pepper, to taste

⅛ teaspoon granulated garlic

1. Preheat the oven to 400°F.

2. Open the can of chickpeas, pour in a strainer, and rinse with cool water. Shake off the excess water and pour onto a tea towel. Gently rub the chickpeas with the towel in a circular motion, discarding any skins that fall off.

3. Place the chickpeas on a parchment-lined baking sheet and allow them to dry to the touch. It is important that the chickpeas are dry before coating them in oil or they will not get crunchy when roasted. This can take up to 30 minutes. Alternatively, you can place the baking sheet with the chickpeas in the oven while it preheats, evaporating the remaining moisture.

4. Once the chickpeas are dry, place them in a small mixing bowl with the olive oil and gently mix with your hands or a wooden spoon until coated. Season with the salt, ground chipotle, and granulated garlic, and gently mix. Return the chickpeas to the baking sheet and spread out in a single layer. If the parchment

paper has absorbed moisture, replace it with fresh paper. Place in the oven to roast for about 40 minutes. Every 15 minutes, remove the baking sheet from the oven and shake in a circular motion to ensure even roasting. The chickpeas are done when they have a medium-brown color and a crispy texture when tasted. Set the tray on a cooling rack until cool to the touch. Store in an airtight container for 5 to 7 days.

Baked Zucchini Chile Chips

Makes about 30 chips

These chips add a zippy accompaniment to any sandwich, salad, or snack time. Best of all, they are totally guilt free, made with a low-calorie, nutritious vegetable and baked to a crisp without oil. The secret is weeping the zucchini prior to baking. By sprinkling with salt and letting the slices stand for ten minutes, the extra moisture is extracted before they are baked. The result is a crunchy, spicy chip.

Prep time: 15 minutes   **Cook time**: 40 minutes

1 medium zucchini, about 7 inches long and 2 to 3 inches in diameter, sliced in $1/8$-inch slices

1 tablespoon white rice flour or coconut flour

$1/4$ teaspoon chile powder or chipotle seasoning

$1/4$ teaspoon granulated garlic

$1/8$ teaspoon finely ground sea salt, plus extra for weeping

pinch black pepper or cayenne pepper

2 tablespoons lemon juice

> **NOTES**
> – What is weeping? Drawing the excess water out of the zucchini slices by sprinkling them with salt and letting them stand for a period of time helps the chips become crispy without the use of oil when they are baked.
> – If you prefer to bake with oil, a teaspoon of olive oil may be massaged on the slices before coating them with the seasoning mix. I would still recommend weeping them prior to this step.

1. Preheat the oven to 350°F and line a baking sheet with parchment paper.

2. Spread the zucchini slices on a cooling rack or strainer placed on a baking sheet (to catch water). Sprinkle the finely ground salt on the slices and repeat on the opposite side. Let sit for 10 minutes to allow excess water to be extracted from the slices.

3. While the zucchini is weeping, combine the flour and chile powder, granulated garlic, salt, and black pepper in a small or medium bowl. Seasoning flour can be doubled if a thicker coating is desired.

4. After 10 minutes, blot the excess water from both sides of the zucchini slices with a tea towel or paper towel. Place the slices in the bowl with the seasoned flour and turn to coat both sides evenly. Gently shake off any excess and place on the baking sheet. Depending on the size of the bowl, this may be done in several batches. Sprinkle each slice with a few drops of lemon juice. Turn over and repeat.

5. Bake for 30 to 40 minutes, turning zucchini over every 10 minutes. Remove from the oven when the slices have reached the desired level of browning and crispness. Add salt to taste, if needed and serve.

Berry Burst Scones

Makes 10 to 12 scones

SF

Are these scones a breakfast or a snack? They have so much going for them nutritionally with all of their plant-based protein, omega-3s, and vitamins and minerals, it seemed certain they would be listed as a breakfast. But it's so easy to grab one on the go as a snack that they ultimately found their home here in the snack section. Either way, they will bring you nutritional love.

Prep time: 15 minutes   **Cook time**: 10 minutes

3 tablespoons golden flaxseed meal

$^1/_2$ cup unsweetened plant-based milk (cashew or almond is best)

3 cups almond meal

$^1/_4$ cup coconut sugar

$^3/_4$ teaspoon baking soda

$^1/_4$ teaspoon finely ground sea salt

$^1/_4$ teaspoon cinnamon

$^1/_2$ cup chopped dried tart cherries

$^1/_2$ cup chopped dried cranberries or blueberries

$^1/_4$ cup walnut, grapeseed, or avocado oil

1 tablespoon vanilla extract

2 teaspoons apple cider vinegar

> **NOTES**
>
> **Substitutions:** Most dried fruits will work well in these scones. My favorite combination is cherry and cranberry, but you can use a blend of several different dried fruits. Just be sure the dried fruit equals 1 cup.
>
> – These scones freeze really well. I suggest making a batch, enjoying a few, and freezing the remaining scones in a zip-top bag. You can take them out one at a time whenever you want one. They thaw beautifully overnight in the refrigerator.
>
> – See my technique for measuring gluten-free flour (page 12) to ensure consistent measurements.

1. Preheat the oven to 350°F. Line two baking sheets with parchment paper.

2. In a small bowl, whisk together the flaxseed meal and plant-based milk. Set aside.

3. In a medium or large mixing bowl, stir together the almond meal, coconut sugar, baking soda, salt, and cinnamon. Once combined, stir in the chopped dried fruit.

4. Add the oil, vanilla, and vinegar to the flax mixture and mix together well. Add the wet ingredients to the dry ingredients and combine thoroughly with a wooden spoon. It will take a minute or two of stirring for the dough to completely blend. If the dough is too dry to combine at this point, 1 to 2 tablespoons of additional plant-based milk may be added.

5. Using a standard ice cream scoop or ¼ to ⅓ cup measuring cup, spoon 6 rounds of the dough on the parchment-lined baking sheets. Make sure the scones are evenly spaced on the baking sheet. Bake for 10 to 13 minutes, until firm to the touch and beginning to show brown peaks. A toothpick inserted in the center of one should come out clean. Remove from the oven and allow to sit on the baking sheet for 2 to 3 minutes, then transfer the scones to a cooling rack. Repeat this step as needed with the remaining dough. The scones will keep up to 1 week in an airtight container in the refrigerator.

Mocha Chocolate Chip Scones

Makes 10 to 12 scones

SF

These scones taste like a doughy chocolate chip cookie laced with subtle notes of coffee. They have just the right flavor combination to satisfy the chocolate and coffee lover at the same time. Watch how fast people gather in your kitchen when these come out of the oven. And thanks to the plant-based protein and other nutrients, they also make a great snack to get you through that *hangry* time.

Prep time: 15 minutes   **Cook time:** 10 minutes

3 tablespoons golden flaxseed meal

¹⁄₂ cup strong coffee (regular or decaffeinated), warm

3 cups almond meal

¹⁄₄ cup coconut sugar

³⁄₄ teaspoon baking soda

¹⁄₄ teaspoon finely ground sea salt

³⁄₄ cup semisweet or dark vegan chocolate chips

¹⁄₄ cup walnut, grapeseed, or avocado oil

1 tablespoon vanilla extract

2 teaspoons apple cider vinegar

> NOTES
> - Mini vegan chocolate chips or chocolate chunks are great substitutions for regular-size chocolate chips.
> - These scones freeze well in a zip-top bag. Remove from the freezer the night before serving and thaw in the refrigerator.
> - See my technique for measuring gluten-free flour (page 12) to ensure consistent measurements.

1. Preheat the oven to 350°F. Line two baking sheets with parchment paper.

2. In a small bowl, whisk together the flaxseed meal and coffee. Set aside.

3. In a medium or large mixing bowl, stir together the almond meal, coconut sugar, baking soda, and salt. Once combined, stir in the chocolate chips.

4. Add the oil, vanilla, and vinegar to the flax mixture and mix together well. Next, add the wet ingredients to the dry ingredients and combine thoroughly with a wooden

spoon. It will take a minute or two of stirring for the dough to completely blend. If the dough is too dry to combine at this point, 1 to 2 tablespoons of additional plant-based milk may be added.

5. Using a standard ice cream scoop or ¼ to ⅓ cup measuring cup, place 6 rounds of the dough on the parchment-lined baking sheets. Make sure the scones are evenly spaced on the baking sheet. Bake for approximately 10 to 13 minutes until firm to the touch and beginning to show brown peaks. A toothpick inserted in the center of one should come out clean. Remove from the oven and allow to sit on the baking sheet for 2 to 3 minutes, then transfer the scones to a cooling rack. Repeat this step as needed with the remaining dough. The scones will keep up to 1 week in an airtight container in the refrigerator.

Cherry Oat Protein Cookies

Servings: 10

I'll be honest: These are my *running out the door and I need a blast of protein* snack. The oats, pepitas, sunflower seeds, and nut butter all deliver protein. Not to mention, the sweet dried cherries keep me coming back for more. These little treats also look great on a platter when entertaining friends and family.

Prep time: 10 minutes   **Cook time**: 15 minutes

1 cup gluten-free quick-cook oats (or substitute regular oats ground into smaller pieces)

⅓ cup diced dried cherries

¼ cup pepitas, lightly chopped

¼ cup sunflower seeds, lightly chopped

3 tablespoons maple syrup

¼ cup cashew or almond butter

½ teaspoon vanilla extract

¼ teaspoon finely ground sea salt

1. Preheat the oven to 325°F. Line a baking sheet with parchment paper.

2. Stir together the gluten-free oats, cherries, pepitas, and sunflower seeds in a medium mixing bowl.

3. Add the maple syrup to the cashew butter in a small glass bowl or saucepan. Using low heat in the microwave for 1 minute or low heat on the stovetop for 2 to 3 minutes, warm until the cashew butter becomes liquid. Add the vanilla and salt and stir well.

4. Add the wet ingredients to the dry ingredients and stir to combine with a wooden spoon. You may need to use your hands to combine the dough. If the mixture seems too dry, add 1 to 2 tablespoons of plant-based milk.

5. Portion about 2 tablespoons of the dough and roll it into a tight ball using your hands. Place the ball of dough on the baking sheet and press into a disk about ⅓ to ½ inch thick. As you press down on the top of the cookie with one hand, shape the side of the cookie with the other. Repeat with the remaining dough.

6. Bake for about 15 minutes for a chewier cookie and 18 minutes for a crispier cookie. Place on a cooling rack for 5 to 10 minutes. Store in an airtight container for 3 to 4 days.

Variation

Substitute sunflower seed butter for the nut butter for a nut-free version. If you have previously baked with sunflower seed butter then you know that under certain conditions it can turn green when heated, but the flavor remains the same.

Secret Spicy Nut Mix

Makes 2 1/2 cups

This is my (no longer) Secret Spicy Nut Mix! Talk about a healthy snack: the good fats, fiber, and vitamin E will make your body smile; the turmeric will make it downright giddy. I always put a bowl out for folks to nibble on before dinner or during the big game.

Prep time: 5 minutes   **Cook time:** 15 minutes

1 tablespoon avocado oil (or substitute walnut, grapeseed, or olive oil)

1/2 teaspoon chile powder

1/2 teaspoon turmeric

1/4 teaspoon cumin

1/4 teaspoon garlic salt

1/4 teaspoon onion powder

1/4 teaspoon finely ground sea salt

1 cup almonds, raw or sprouted

1 cup cashews, raw

1/4 cup walnuts, chopped

1/4 cup pepitas, sprouted (shelled pumpkin seeds)

> **NOTE**
> – Sometimes when I'm feeling extra spicy I like to add 1/8 teaspoon of cayenne pepper to give the flavor an extra kick.

1. Preheat the oven to 350°F. Line a baking sheet with parchment paper.

2. In a small bowl combine the oil, chile powder, turmeric, cumin, garlic salt, onion powder, and salt. Whisk together until thoroughly combined.

3. In a medium bowl mix the almonds, cashews, walnuts, and pepitas. Pour the seasoned oil over the nuts and stir with a wooden spoon until evenly coated.

4. Spread evenly on the baking sheet and bake for 15 minutes. About halfway through cooking time remove the pan from the oven and turn the nut mixture over to ensure even browning. Cooking time may be shortened or extended by a couple of minutes if more or less crispiness is desired. Once the nuts have cooled, store them in an airtight container for up to 5 to 7 days.

Apricot Nut Bites

Makes 10 to 12 bites

With the warm scent of cinnamon, these no-bake energy bites are chewy and buttery. The apricot and coconut pair well and don't overwhelm the vanilla. They are perfect for that little sweet snack in between meals. My favorite way to serve them is as a fancy finger food for a wine tasting. Arrange them on a decorative platter, sprinkle with a bit of coconut, and watch them disappear!

Prep time: 10 minutes   **Cook time:** none

1 cup unsweetened shredded coconut, divided

½ cup dried apricots, about 15 apricots (moist and tender fruits work better than hard and dry ones)

¼ cup almond meal

1 teaspoon vanilla extract

⅛ teaspoon cinnamon

⅛ teaspoon finely ground sea salt (optional; add if apricots are too tart)

1. Add ½ cup coconut and the apricots to a food processor and blend until both are broken down, about 1 minute.

2. Add the almond meal, vanilla, cinnamon, and optional salt. Blend until smooth and completely combined.

3. Place the remaining coconut on a plate. Scoop 1 tablespoon of the mixture, roll into a ball with your hands, then roll in the shredded coconut to coat. Repeat with the remaining mixture. These may be eaten immediately or after refrigeration for a firmer bite. Store in an airtight container in the refrigerator for up to 1 week.

Tip: If your coconut is not shredded into fine pieces suitable for coating your bites, place all of the coconut in the food processor and blend until it is pulverized. Remove ¼ cup of coconut for coating balls, set aside, and follow the recipe starting with step 1.

CHAPTER 8

Appetizers
and
Small Plates

Broccoli with Olive and Fig Tapenade

Servings: 4 to 6

Gently coating steamed broccoli with the generous flavors and colors of this olive tapenade turns a mundane side dish into a culinary pleasure. The result is a savory dish with spicy notes and subtle sweetness. I recommend preparing extra tapenade to use as a dipping oil for fresh bread, crostini, or warm slices of Rosmarino Flatbread (page 100).

Prep time: 5 minutes   **Cook time:** 5 minutes

2 medium crowns fresh broccoli

¹⁄₃ cup extra virgin olive oil

8 medium pimento stuffed green olives

1 medium Calimyrna dried fig

¹⁄₄ teaspoon dried crushed red pepper, to taste

¹⁄₈ teaspoon granulated garlic

finely ground sea salt and black pepper, to taste

1. Chop the broccoli florets and stems into 1- to 2-inch pieces. If using stems, peel them first, as this will make them tender. Steam the broccoli in a countertop steamer or steamer basket in a pan on the stovetop for about 5 minutes or until fork-tender yet still firm.

2. Place the olive oil, olives, fig, and red pepper in a food processor and chop until small pieces remain. Scrape the sides and add the granulated garlic, salt, and pepper, to taste. Pulse briefly to mix thoroughly. Alternatively, ingredients may be finely chopped and mixed by hand.

3. Place the hot broccoli in a bowl, dollop with 3 to 4 tablespoons of tapenade, and turn gently to coat. Add more tapenade to taste. Serve on a platter or in a long bowl, season with salt and pepper, and serve immediately.

Variation

Substitute 1 to 2 tablespoons sun-dried tomatoes for the figs, if desired.

Roasted Asparagus with Avocado Cream

Servings: 4

This recipe not only serves as a rich side dish, it is a conversation starter. The combination of roasted asparagus and fresh garlic and sweet corn drizzled with a cilantro avocado cream yields a flavor experience like no other. And because it is a unique dish that tastes phenomenal either hot out of the oven or chilled, you have a large number of pairing options. Plus, it can be ready in less than 30 minutes!

Prep time: 15 minutes   **Cook time:** 12 minutes

½ large avocado, peeled and pitted

¼ cup unsweetened plant-based milk (I use cashew milk, which is not nut-free)

2 tablespoons fresh cilantro

1 tablespoon lemon juice

⅛ teaspoon finely ground sea salt

1 cup sweet corn kernels (drained and dried if using canned corn)

6 large cloves fresh garlic, minced

3 tablespoons olive oil, divided

1 pound fresh asparagus spears, washed and dried

NOTES

- If chilling asparagus, place the avocado cream in an airtight container and refrigerate as well.

- To dry the vegetables, first wash them and then place each vegetable on a separate tea towel and gently blot to remove excess moisture. Set aside to dry for 15 to 20 minutes. It is important to remove all moisture or the vegetables will steam in the oven instead of roasting.

---

1. Preheat the oven to 475°F. Line a baking sheet with parchment paper and set aside.

2. Place the avocado, plant-based milk, cilantro, lemon juice, and salt in food processor or high-speed blender and mix until smooth. Cover and set aside.

3. In a small mixing bowl, place the corn, minced garlic, and 2 tablespoons olive oil and stir gently to combine. Set aside.

4. Spread the asparagus in a single layer on the baking sheet lined with parchment paper. Drizzle with 1 tablespoon olive oil. Roll the asparagus back and forth with the palm of your hand to coat evenly in oil. Sprinkle the corn mixture over the asparagus. Place in the oven for 12 minutes, until it begins to brown. Remove from the oven and allow to cool for 5 minutes or refrigerate for 15 to 20 minutes to chill completely. To serve, drizzle with the avocado cream and enjoy.

Kicked Up Vegan Mac and Cheese

Servings: 12

I enlisted the help of cauliflower to make this sauce velvety smooth and creamy. Plus, it is an amazing secret ingredient that carries none of the vegetable's flavor to the sauce. This dish is so flexible, you can adjust the seasoning as desired. It calls for cayenne pepper to bring the heat, but you can omit it if you want a more traditional version. Want to enhance the spiciness? Add a small can of drained chopped green chilies or substitute the vegan cheddar with vegan pepper jack. Have fun with it!

Prep time: 25 minutes   **Cook time**: 35 minutes

12 ounces gluten-free penne or elbow pasta

1/2 large head cauliflower, cut into florets

1/2 cup raw cashews, soaked

1/4 cup olive oil

8 medium cloves fresh garlic, minced

1/3 cup minced sweet onion

1/4 cup arrowroot

3/4 cup unsweetened cashew milk or mild tasting plant-based milk

1/4 to 1/2 teaspoon finely ground cayenne pepper, to taste

1/2 teaspoon finely ground sea salt

1/4 teaspoon finely ground black pepper

3/4 teaspoon fresh lemon juice

1 1/2 cups shredded vegan cheddar cheese

1 cup gluten-free bread crumbs

vegan butter (optional for bread crumbs)

> **NOTES**
> - For an oil-free version, replace the olive oil in the recipe with vegetable broth or water. See instructions for sautéing without oil on page 17.
>
> - Soaking cashews is required prior to starting this recipe. See page 17 for quick-soak or overnight-soak instructions.
>
> - When prepared according to the following directions, this recipe makes a casserole-style macaroni and cheese. For a creamier version, I would suggest preparing 1 1/2 times the sauce. Accordingly, the oven temperature should be increased to 350°F for the entirety of the cooking time.

1. Cook the pasta according to the directions on the package and drain. While the pasta is cooking, steam the cauliflower florets in a countertop steamer or steamer basket in a pan on the stovetop for about 20 minutes or until fork-tender. If you are using the quick-soak method for the cashews, do so at this time as well.

2. While the pasta and cauliflower are cooking and the cashews are soaking, heat a medium saucepan on the stovetop with the olive oil. When the olive oil is hot,

add the minced garlic and onion. Sauté until the garlic is golden brown and the onion is translucent, about 5 minutes.

3. Leave the garlic and onion mixture on medium heat and whisk in the arrowroot until blended, about 1 minute. Add the cashew milk, whisking about 1 to 2 minutes to blend. Remove from the heat.

4. Add the steamed cauliflower, prepared cashews, and garlic-onion mixture to a high-speed blender. Gently pulse. Pause and remove the lid to stir manually if the blades are having difficulty spinning. Continue doing this until enough liquid is generated to allow free movement of the blades. Blend on high until smooth, about 2 to 3 minutes. Add the cayenne pepper, salt, black pepper, and lemon juice. Blend until smooth. Taste and add additional salt, black pepper, and lemon juice if desired.

5. Preheat the oven to 325°F. Grease a 13 x 9-inch glass baking dish with olive oil.

6. Place the cooked pasta in a large mixing bowl and gently stir in the sauce with a spatula or wooden spoon. Add the cheese and gently mix to combine. Pour the mixture into the greased baking dish. Flatten the mixture with a spatula and sprinkle with the gluten-free bread crumbs. You can add some melted vegan butter to the bread crumbs before sprinkling for extra buttery flavor, if desired.

7. Cover with aluminum foil and bake for 15 minutes. Uncover, and increase the temperature to 350°F. Bake an additional 15 to 20 minutes until the bread crumbs are brown and the dish begins to bubble. Remove from the oven and place the pan on a cooling rack for 5 to 10 minutes before serving.

8. Leftovers may be stored in a sealed container in the refrigerator. To reheat the Mac and Cheese, place it in a pan with 1 to 2 tablespoons of plant-based milk per cup of Mac and Cheese. Warm over low heat and gently stir. This same process will also work well with a bowl in the microwave, using medium-high power.

Charred Brussels Sprouts with Horseradish Cream

Servings: 4

When I need a powerhouse side, this recipe is my go-to. If you are serving up a mild main or want a veggie with personality, these Brussels sprouts deliver. The char on the sprouts gives the dish just what it needs to offset the vegetable's earthiness. And the dichotomy of the pungent horseradish and the creamy base makes for the ultimate drizzle. I peel some outer leaves from the Brussels sprouts before roasting to add extra little crispies on top.

Prep time: 10 minutes   **Cook time:** 20 to 25 minutes

1 pound Brussels sprouts

1 to 2 teaspoons olive oil (use lemon juice for an oil-free option)

½ teaspoon coarse sea salt

¼ teaspoon black pepper, divided

1 cup raw cashews, soaked

½ cup water (more or less may be used to achieve desired thickness)

¼ cup prepared horseradish

1 tablespoon lemon juice

½ teaspoon finely ground sea salt

⅛ teaspoon granulated garlic

> **NOTE**
> – Soaking cashews is required prior to starting this recipe. See page 17 for quick-soak or overnight-soak instructions.

1. Preheat the oven to 450°F. Line a large baking sheet with parchment paper.

2. Wash the Brussels sprouts and then place them in a single layer on a tea towel to dry. Once dry, cut off the bottom of the core, remove yellow leaves, and cut in half lengthwise.

3. Place the Brussels sprouts in a medium mixing bowl. Drizzle the vegetables with oil, and stir gently to coat. Add the salt and ⅛ teaspoon pepper and stir again to coat. Spread out the sprout halves in a single layer on the baking sheet with cut side down.

4. Reduce the heat in the oven to 400°F and place the baking sheet in the oven. Bake for 20 to 25 minutes,

until the Brussels sprouts are lightly charred and crisp on the outside and fork-tender in the center. Carefully observe the sprouts toward the end of the baking time, as they tend to brown quickly. Cooking time will vary based on the size of your sprouts. After removing from the oven allow the sprouts to cool for 2 to 3 minutes before plating.

5. While the Brussels sprouts are baking, make the horseradish cream. Place the soaked cashews, water, and prepared horseradish in a blender or food processor. Some types of prepared horseradish have more liquid than others, so I recommend reserving 2 tablespoons of the water and adding the water incrementally so the cream does not become too thin. Pulse a few times and begin to blend on low speed. Add the remaining water, if necessary. Add the lemon juice, salt, granulated garlic, and ⅛ teaspoon pepper. Pulse a few times, then blend on high speed until smooth, about 3 to 4 minutes, stopping periodically to scrape the sides.

6. To serve, transfer the sprouts to a platter or individual plates and drizzle with the horseradish cream. Serve extra cream on the side.

Lemon Garlic Oven Fries

Servings: 6

These crisp yet oil-free fries take the guilt out of a guilty pleasure! Who would have thought that four ingredients could taste so delicious yet complex? Bring that homestyle love to your next plant-based burger, sandwich, or salad with a flavorful fancy flair.

Prep time: 10 minutes   **Cook time:** 30 minutes

3 to 4 tablespoons fresh lemon juice

3 tablespoons minced garlic, about 5 to 6 large cloves

1/4 teaspoon finely ground sea salt, plus more for seasoning cooked fries

dash black pepper, plus more for seasoning cooked fries

2 to 2 1/2 pounds all-purpose potatoes, such as Yukon Gold, Russet, or butter (about 5 medium potatoes)

3 to 4 tablespoons minced fresh Italian parsley

NOTE

– Prepare your ingredients the night before for ease while cooking. Mix the potatoes and lemon juice mixture together and store in an airtight bag or container in the refrigerator. Then all you have to do is bake them in the oven the next day!

---

1. Preheat the oven to 450°F. Line two baking sheets with parchment paper.

2. In a small bowl, place the lemon juice, garlic, salt, and pepper. Set aside.

3. Leaving the skin on, thoroughly clean and dry the potatoes and cut them lengthwise in 1/4-inch wedges.

4. Place the potatoes in a large mixing bowl and pour the lemon juice–garlic mixture on the potatoes. Mix well using your hands. Alternatively, strain the garlic from the lemon juice before adding to the potatoes and set aside.

5. Spread the potatoes in a single layer on parchment-lined baking sheets, making sure not to overcrowd the potatoes. Sprinkle with additional salt and pepper to taste, if desired. Bake for 20 minutes then turn the potatoes over with a metal spatula, add more salt and pepper and the reserved garlic (if you prefer it lightly browned), if desired, and return to the oven for an additional 10 minutes. Remove from the oven when the potatoes have lightly puffed and browned to the desired crispness. Garnish with the garlic, if not used in step 4, and fresh parsley. Serve warm.

Eggplant Caponata

Makes approximately 6 cups

Caponata is a traditional Sicilian dish that takes many forms, and while many versions have overlapping ingredients, such as eggplant, onions, and garlic, some recipes will add or remove various other items like olives, capers, or sugar. My version has no added sugar as it maximizes the full expression of the naturally occurring sweetness in the vegetables. I also like to make it with capers and red pepper flakes for a little extra zest and zip. *Mangia*!

Prep time: 15 minutes   **Cook time:** 45 minutes

¼ cup olive oil

2 medium eggplants, diced to ¼- to ½-inch cubes

1 medium onion, diced to ¼- to ½-inch cubes

1 medium green pepper, diced to ¼- to ½-inch cubes

3 stalks celery, diced to ¼- to ½-inch cubes

1 small bulb garlic, minced (about 5 to 7 cloves)

¾ cup Kalamata olives, pitted

¾ cup green olives, pitted

8 ounces tomato sauce

6 ounces tomato paste

2 to 3 tablespoons red wine vinegar, to taste

¼ teaspoon dried oregano

a few drops of hot sauce, to taste

finely ground sea salt, to taste

black pepper, to taste

baguette slices, crackers, fresh bread, or a bed of greens, for serving

1. Pour the olive oil into a large skillet over medium heat. Once the oil and pan are hot, add the diced vegetables and garlic and sauté until the vegetables are translucent, about 30 minutes.

2. Chop the olives lengthwise, some in half and some in quarters.

3. Add the olives, tomato sauce, tomato paste, and vinegar to the pan with the sautéed vegetables. Mix well, cover, and reduce heat to low. Simmer at least 15 minutes or until the eggplant is very tender, stirring frequently.

4. Stir in the oregano, hot sauce, salt, and pepper.

5. Serve with baguette slices, crackers, or fresh bread, or over a bed of greens. This dish can be enjoyed warm, at room temperature, or cold. After a day the flavors will develop, but it can be served immediately, as well. Store in an airtight container in the refrigerator. This dish will keep at least 1 week.

NOTE

– When selecting eggplant, it is important to pick one that feels heavy in your hand. The skin should be smooth and unblemished and the stem should still be green.

Creamy White Beans and Rice

Servings: 4

I love to serve this rich and flavorful dish in a bowl alongside a colorful salad loaded with fresh veggies. It works perfectly as a side dish, but has enough protein and fiber that it is hearty enough to be a main course. The creaminess of the white beans makes this dish a delightful alternative to traditional black beans and rice.

Prep time: 5 minutes   **Cook time:** 15 minutes (including rice)

1 cup uncooked jasmine rice or 3 ½ cups cooked rice (long grain white sticky rice may be substituted)

1 teaspoon olive oil, or saute in vegetable broth for an oil-free option (page 17)

⅓ cup diced sweet onion

½ teaspoon finely ground sea salt

¼ teaspoon chile powder

¼ teaspoon onion powder

⅛ teaspoon cayenne pepper, to taste

1 (15-ounce) can white beans, drained (Great Northern are best)

¼ cup cashew milk, or mild-tasting plant-based milk for nut-free option

1 tablespoon nutritional yeast

¼ cup chopped fresh cilantro

1. Prepare the rice. Add 1 cup uncooked rice and 1 ¾ cups water to a medium saucepan. Uncovered, bring to a boil over high heat. When the liquid is at a rolling boil, stir and reduce the heat to a simmer. Cover and cook 12 to 15 minutes. Once the liquid is evaporated, stir the rice periodically to prevent burning. The rice is done when sticky and tender. Remove from the heat and let stand for 3 or 4 minutes. Use a fork to fluff the rice before serving.

2. While the rice is simmering, prepare the beans. Heat the oil or vegetable broth in a medium or large skillet over medium heat. Add the onion to the pan and season with the salt, chile powder, onion powder, and cayenne pepper. Stir to combine the seasonings with the onion. Sauté until the onion begins to turn translucent and the seasonings are fragrant, stirring occasionally, about 2 to 3 minutes.

3. Add the beans to the skillet. Stir to combine the beans and the onion mixture and continue sautéing until the beans are warm, about 1 minute. When stirring, gently scoop and turn the beans to avoid breaking or mashing.

4. Add the cashew milk to the pan. Stir until the cashew milk is warm, about 1 minute. Add the nutritional yeast and stir to combine. Reduce the heat to a very gentle simmer. Once the nutritional yeast has dissolved, about 3 to 4 minutes, stir in the cilantro and continue cooking for an additional 1 to 2 minutes while stirring. Serve immediately over rice.

Sautéed Baby Bok Choy Over White Bean Puree

Servings: 8

This recipe is the perfect side dish for the foodie dinner host in you. Combining the earthy flavors of bok choy, garlic, and onion, served over a creamy puree, this dish will impress your palate as much as your guests'. Dress up the plate with bok choy rosettes and a sprig of rosemary for an extra-elegant touch.

Prep time: 5 minutes   **Cook time:** 15 minutes

1 ½ teaspoons olive oil, divided, or saute in vegetable broth for an oil-free option (page 17)

²/₃ cup diced sweet onion, divided

2 tablespoons minced garlic, divided

1 teaspoon dried rosemary leaves

³/₄ teaspoon finely ground sea salt, divided

dash black pepper

½ cup unsweetened cashew milk, or mild-tasting plant-based milk for nut-free option

1 (15-ounce) can cannellini beans, rinsed and drained

4 teaspoons coconut or liquid aminos, divided

10 to 12 heads baby bok choy, core removed and chopped in 1-inch slices

1. Heat ½ teaspoon oil in a small skillet over medium heat. Add ⅓ cup onion, 1 tablespoon minced garlic, rosemary, ½ teaspoon salt, and pepper. Stir to combine the seasoning with the onion and garlic. Sauté until the onion begins to turn translucent and the garlic begins to brown, about 8 minutes, stirring occasionally. If the seasoning sticks to the bottom of the pan, 2 tablespoons of the cashew milk may be used to deglaze the pan.

2. Add the mixture from the pan, cashew milk, beans, and 2 teaspoons coconut aminos to a high-speed blender. Blend on high speed until smooth. Set aside.

3. Heat the remaining teaspoon of oil in a large skillet (preferably one with higher sides) over medium heat. Add the remaining ⅓ cup onion, 1 tablespoon minced garlic, and ¼ teaspoon salt. Sauté until the onion begins to turn translucent and the garlic begins to brown, about 8 minutes, stirring occasionally.

4. Add the bok choy to the pan and combine with the onions and garlic. Add 2 teaspoons coconut aminos and stir gently. Sauté until the bok choy becomes tender but still bright green, about 1 to 2 minutes, stirring occasionally.

5. To plate, spoon about ¼ cup of white bean puree onto a plate and top with the baby bok choy. Serve immediately.

Baked Ricotta Crostini

Servings: 32

These pretty, cheesy, toasty appetizers go fast when they hit the table. The light and pillowy herbed cheese is the perfect treat for holding in one hand and a glass of wine in the other. Plus, these are kid-friendly!

Prep time: 5 minutes   **Cook time:** 15 minutes

1 baguette, approximately
2 inches wide by 1 inch high and
16 inches long

2 cups Vegan Ricotta Cheese,
with herbs (page 81), at room
temperature

minced green olives and tomato
for topping (optional; use only
the flesh of the tomato to avoid
fluid leaking onto the crostini)

1. Preheat the oven to 350°F. Line a baking sheet with parchment paper.

2. Slice the baguette into ½-inch slices. Place the bread slices on a baking sheet and toast in the oven until lightly brown, about 8 to 10 minutes. Alternatively, for a version that is not oil-free, lightly coat each slice of bread with olive oil before toasting in the oven.

3. Once lightly browned, remove the bread slices from the oven. Increase the oven temperature to 425°F.

4. Cover each toasted bread slice with about 1 tablespoon ricotta cheese. It should be about ¼-inch thick. Return the ricotta crostini to the parchment-lined baking sheet, spacing them at least 1 inch apart. Bake for about 5 to 7 minutes or until ricotta begins to turn light brown.

5. Remove from the oven and place the crostini on a cooling rack for 3 to 5 minutes. To serve, top with the minced green olives and tomatoes, if desired. This may be served hot but also can be served at room temperature or after refrigerating.

Tip: Short on time? Pick up a package of prepared gluten-free crostini at the store and skip steps 1 and 2.

Veggie Shooters

I love this party-perfect appetizer. It checks all of the boxes: pretty presentation, allows for mess-free mingling, tastes delicious, and is easy to prepare. You can customize this appetizer with your favorite colorful and seasonal vegetables. Plus, the plant-based ranch dressing means you and your guests stay light on your feet.

Prep time: 10 minutes   **Cook time:** none

1 large red bell pepper

1 large yellow bell pepper

2 large carrots

1 English cucumber

1 kohlrabi or jicama

Ranch Dressing (page 73)

> **NOTES**
> – The glasses I used are about 3½ inches tall and 1½ inches in diameter. Any small clear glass will do.
> – The dressing can be made a day in advance for easy preparation. I use the minimum amount of fluid in the recipe to create a thicker dressing that adheres to the veggies when they are removed from the glass.

Tips:

– To prepare the bell pepper, cut off the top and the bottom and remove the core. Then slice into vertical strips.

– To prepare the kohlrabi or jicama, after peeling, cut into ¼-inch-thick circles. Then use the center of the circles to get the tallest strips when cutting. Reserve unused strips for snacking on or topping a salad.

1. Wash, dry, and peel (if needed) the vegetables. Cut the vegetables in 4- to 5-inch strips about ¼ inch wide. The size of your vegetable strips could vary depending on your serving glass. You want the vegetables to be tall enough that that they exceed the glass height but not so tall that the glass is top heavy.

2. Place the dressing in the bottom third of each glass.

3. Arrange the vegetables in the glasses and serve.

Buffalo Cauliflower

Servings: 6 to 8

This Buffalo Cauliflower recipe will score major points on game day. The coating for these bite-size party pleasers offers just the right delicacy and seasoning to emulate the traditional recipe. Buffalo wing aficionados have been amazed at the similarity in taste and texture and usually go back for a second round!

Prep time: 15 minutes   **Cook time:** 25 minutes

³/₄ cup unsweetened plant-based milk

³/₄ cup white rice flour

¹/₂ teaspoon onion powder

¹/₂ teaspoon garlic powder

¹/₂ teaspoon finely ground sea salt

¹/₄ teaspoon paprika

1 medium (about 1 pound) head cauliflower cut into small florets, about 3¹/₂ to 4 cups

²/₃ cup hot pepper sauce such as Frank's Red Hot Original

2 tablespoons white vinegar (see tip about gluten-free)

2 teaspoons tahini (or substitute almond or cashew butter for a non nut-free version)

¹/₂ teaspoon coconut aminos (or gluten-free soy sauce for a non–soy free version)

Ranch Dressing (page 73) for serving

carrots and celery sticks, for serving

> **NOTE**
> – See my technique for measuring gluten-free flour (page 12) to ensure consistent measurements.

1. Preheat the oven to 425°F. Line a baking sheet with parchment paper.

2. In a medium bowl whisk together the plant-based milk, rice flour, onion powder, garlic powder, salt, and paprika until combined. Place the cauliflower into the batter and gently stir to coat.

3. Remove the cauliflower florets from the bowl with a slotted spoon to remove excess batter. Place in a single layer on the baking sheet, making sure they do not touch. Bake for 15 minutes. Remove the baking sheet from the oven and turn the cauliflower florets. Bake for an additional 5 to 7 minutes or until golden brown and the breading is firm and dry.

4. While the cauliflower bakes, combine the pepper sauce, white vinegar, tahini, and coconut aminos in a small saucepan and place on the stovetop over low heat. Whisk together while warming. Once the sauce is warm, remove it from the heat and cover.

5. Remove the cauliflower from the oven when it is done but leave the oven on. Place the cauliflower in a medium bowl and cover with the buffalo sauce. Gently turn the cauliflower in the sauce until coated. Return the cauliflower to the baking sheet and return to the oven for an additional 3 to 5 minutes until warm.

6. Serve immediately with your favorite dipping sauce or my Ranch Dressing (page 73) and accompany with carrot and celery sticks.

Tip: Is distilled white vinegar gluten-free? According to the Vinegar Institute, distilled white vinegar is considered gluten-free if it is made from apples, grapes, corn, or rice. Always be sure to check the label.

Fruit and Nut Cheese Log

Servings: varies (makes a log 7 inches long by 2 ½ inches wide and high)

Let's get retro! In the 1970s, no party table was complete without a cheese log and a spread of crackers. What's old is new again, and folks are creating these logs with different herbs, fruits, and/or nuts. Loaded with dried fruits and coated with chopped nuts, this plant-based cheese will be a tasty snack, pre-dinner appetizer, or accompaniment to a wine tasting.

Prep time: 10 minutes (not including refrigeration or soaking time)   **Cook time:** none

2 cups raw cashews, soaked

3 tablespoons lemon juice

2 ½ teaspoons apple cider vinegar

1 ½ teaspoons vanilla extract

½ teaspoon finely ground sea salt

¼ cup diced dried pineapple

¼ cup diced dried papaya or dried apricot

¼ cup diced dried tart cherries or diced dried cranberries

½ cup chopped walnut, pecans, or almonds

water crackers, rice crackers or other neutral crackers, for serving

fresh fruit slices, such as apples or pears, for serving

fresh vegetable slices, such as jicama, celery or carrots, for serving

> **NOTES**
> – Soaking cashews is required prior to starting this recipe. See page 17 for quick-soak or overnight-soak instructions. If you are soaking the cashews by the hot water method soak the nuts for about 2 hours. The soaking time is a bit longer than recommended for other recipes in the book.

1. Place the cashews in a food processor and pulse until broken into small pieces. Add the lemon juice, vinegar, vanilla, and salt and blend until smooth, about 1 to 2 minutes. As you are blending, the ingredients will form a ball. Pause occasionally to scrape the sides and bottom of the food processor and flatten out the ball to continue blending.

2. Once smooth, add the dried fruits to the cashew mixture in the food processor and pulse a few times to mix together.

3. Place a piece of plastic wrap in a small bowl. Empty the contents of the food processor into the bowl. Gather the edges of the plastic wrap and pull together to form a ball or log. Refrigerate for 1 hour or more, until firm enough to handle.

4. Place the chopped nuts on a flat plate or tray. Remove the cheese ball from the refrigerator. Remove the plastic wrap and form into a log if you have not done so already. Alternatively, you can leave it as a ball and serve a cheese ball instead. Gently roll the cheese in nuts to coat.

5. Serve the cheese log immediately with crackers, fruit, or vegetables. The cheese log will keep in the refrigerator for about 5 days. It may also be frozen for 4 to 6 weeks. Before serving, thaw in the refrigerator overnight.

CHAPTER 9

Mains and Big Plates

Black Beans and Cauliflower Rice

Servings: 4 main dishes or 6 side servings

This zippy dish is lower in carbs and higher in nutrients than traditional black beans and white rice. It is very versatile and makes a great main course, tasty side, or the perfect filling for a burrito. For a milder version, I suggest omitting the cayenne pepper and pickled jalapeño slices, substituting cilantro for the parsley, and adding 2 teaspoons of fresh lime juice. For a spicier version, add ¼ teaspoon chile powder, ¼ teaspoon granulated garlic, and a pinch of thyme after adding the black beans. If you want more spice you can add more in quarter-teaspoon increments.

Prep time: 10 minutes   **Cook time:** 15 minutes

2 tablespoons olive oil, or saute in vegetable broth or water for an oil-free option (page 17)

½ cup diced sweet onion, about half a large onion

3 cloves fresh garlic, minced

½ cup diced red bell pepper, about 1 medium pepper

¼ teaspoon ground cayenne pepper, to taste

sea salt and black pepper, to taste

3 tablespoons diced pickled jalapeño slices (may be omitted for a milder version)

3 rounded cups prepared riced cauliflower (about 1 medium head cauliflower)

1 (15-ounce) can black beans, rinsed and drained

½ cup chopped fresh parsley or cilantro

1. Heat the oil in a medium or large skillet over medium heat. Add the onion and garlic to the olive oil, and sauté until golden. Add the bell pepper, cayenne pepper, salt, and black pepper to the onion and garlic and stir to combine. Continue sautéing until the onion begins to turn translucent, stirring occasionally, about 5 minutes. Add the pickled jalapeño and stir.

2. Pour the cauliflower on top of the vegetables and sprinkle well with salt and black pepper. Mix, then add more salt and black pepper, to taste. Continue cooking about 5 to 7 minutes or until the cauliflower is soft b~ut not mushy. After three minutes, use a spatula to flip the rice and stir.

3. Add the black beans and cook an additional 2 minutes or until the beans are warm and gently softened. Add the parsley or cilantro, mix well, and serve. Leftovers may be refrigerated for 3 to 4 days and reheated. To reheat, place covered in the microwave for 1 to 2 minutes on medium power or in a skillet on the stovetop for 5 to 7 minutes over medium heat while stirring intermittently.

How to Rice Cauliflower

Cut the cauliflower head into florets and remove the thick core. Add the florets to the food processor and pulse in small batches until riced. Do not pulse too much or the cauliflower will start to puree. Empty the riced cauliflower into a large bowl and repeat as needed. If there are uncut pieces of the core, remove them and discard. Alternatively, a box grater may be used to rice cauliflower.

Eggplant Cauliflower Dirty Rice

Makes approximately 8 cups

This eggplant and cauliflower low-carb and plant-based dish is a consistent favorite on my blog and one of the most requested dishes in my home. Combining accents of both Cajun and Creole cuisine, the flavors in this satisfying meal are bursting through to the very last bite on your plate.

Prep time: 30 minutes   **Cook time:** 40 minutes

¼ cup plus 2 tablespoons olive oil, divided

¼ teaspoon garlic powder

½ teaspoon red pepper flakes

1 ¼ teaspoons finely ground sea salt, divided

½ teaspoon finely ground black pepper, divided

1 medium eggplant, about 1 pound diced into ½-inch cubes

2 cloves fresh garlic, minced

1 cup diced white onion, about 1 large onion

2 stalks celery, diced, about ¾ cup

½ cup diced green bell pepper, about 1 medium pepper

½ cup diced red bell pepper, about 1 medium pepper

3 rounded cups riced cauliflower, about 1 medium head cauliflower

1 teaspoon dried thyme

¼ teaspoon cayenne

¼ teaspoon paprika

(continued on the following page)

1. Preheat the oven to 400°F. Line a baking sheet with parchment paper.

2. In a large bowl combine ¼ cup olive oil with the garlic powder, red pepper flakes, ¼ teaspoon salt, and ¼ teaspoon black pepper and stir to combine. Add the eggplant to the seasoned oil and toss to coat well. Spread the eggplant pieces in a single layer on a baking sheet. Bake for 40 minutes, removing the baking sheet after 20 minutes to flip the eggplant to the other side. Once done, remove from the oven and leave the eggplant on the baking sheet until ready to add to the vegetable mixture.

3. While the eggplant is roasting, prepare the riced cauliflower, if needed. For instructions see page 173.

4. In a large skillet warm 2 tablespoons olive oil over medium heat. Add the garlic to the olive oil and when the garlic begins to sizzle add the onion, celery, and bell peppers. Sauté the vegetables until the onion begins to turn translucent, about 5 to 8 minutes.

5. Add the cauliflower rice to the vegetables. Mix together with a wooden spoon or spatula. Sprinkle with the remaining 1 teaspoon salt and ¼ teaspoon black pepper and stir. Add the dried thyme to the mixture

¼ teaspoon cumin

¼ teaspoon ground chipotle chile pepper (less, for a milder option, but replace with equal parts cumin)

> **NOTE**
> – If a milder dish is desired, the amounts of cayenne and chipotle peppers can be reduced. If the ground chipotle pepper is reduced, replace it with an equal amount of cumin.

by rubbing it between your fingers when adding. Add the cayenne, paprika, cumin, and chipotle and stir the mixture well.

6. Continue sautéing the vegetables about 5 to 7 minutes or until the cauliflower is soft but not mushy. Add the eggplant to the mixture and gently stir to combine. Leave on the heat just long enough to warm the eggplant if it has cooled. Serve immediately as a side dish or an entrée. This keeps well in the refrigerator in an airtight container for 3 to 4 days and can easily be reheated. To reheat, place covered in the microwave for 1 to 2 minutes on medium power or in a skillet on the stovetop for 5 to 7 minutes over medium heat, while stirring intermittently.

Classic Sloppy Joes

Servings: 7 to 8 Joes

Tangy on the taste buds and hearty in the belly, these scrumptious sandwiches will satisfy the healthiest of appetites with generous amounts of protein and an abundance of flavor. I used carrots and red bell peppers instead of adding sugar to bring that classic sweet component while increasing nutrients. The filling can be served on gluten-free buns or baguette, in a wrap, or over pasta.

Prep time: 10 minutes   **Cook time:** 20 minutes

1 cup dried lentils, rinsed in cold water

2 cups vegetable broth

1 teaspoon avocado, olive, or refined coconut oil, or vegetable broth or water for an oil-free option (page 17)

1 cup diced red bell pepper, about $^3/_4$ large pepper

$^1/_2$ cup diced onion, about $^1/_2$ large onion

1 cup grated carrot

1 $^1/_2$ teaspoons paprika

1 $^1/_8$ teaspoons garlic powder

1 teaspoon chile powder

$^1/_2$ to $^3/_4$ teaspoon finely ground sea salt, to taste

dash black pepper

1 $^1/_2$ cups tomato sauce (most of a 15-ounce can)

1 tablespoon plus 2 teaspoons prepared mustard

1 tablespoon apple cider vinegar

> **NOTE**
> – For Sloppy Joes with more bite use green lentils. For a softer sandwich filling use red lentils and mash the mixture with a potato masher 5 to 6 times before serving.

1. Place the lentils and broth in a medium saucepan. Bring to a gentle simmer and cover with a tilted lid for about 20 minutes. Most liquid should be absorbed and the lentils will be soft.

2. In a large skillet, warm the oil over medium heat. Sauté the pepper, onion, and carrot for about 7 to 8 minutes, until the onion is translucent.

3. Add the paprika, garlic powder, chile powder, salt, and pepper to the vegetables, mix well, and cook for an additional 1 to 2 minutes to release flavors.

4. Stir the tomato sauce into the vegetable mixture. Then add the mustard and apple cider vinegar. Continue stirring over medium heat until the sauce is warm.

Gently fold the lentils into the sauce with a wooden spoon or spatula. Remove from heat. Serve on a gluten-free roll or baguette.

5. Store the leftovers in a sealed container in the refrigerator. It will keep for 3 to 5 days. Reheat the leftovers in a skillet on the stovetop. If added moisture is desired, add a tablespoon of tomato sauce or vegetable broth, as needed.

Zesty Buckwheat Burgers

Makes 9 burgers

Buckwheat gives these burgers their hearty substance and chewy texture like a traditional burger. This gratifying burger alternative is zesty but paired back in order not to overwhelm any toppings or condiments. Plus, it is entirely plant-based and free from grains, nuts, beans, and soy. And you can bake these burgers or fry them, if you prefer. Look no farther, your burger days are back!

Prep time: 40 minutes   **Cook time:** 30 minutes

1 ½ pounds butternut squash

2 tablespoons olive oil, divided

1 ½ teaspoons finely ground sea salt, divided

1 ½ teaspoons paprika, divided

1 ½ teaspoons chile powder, divided

1 cup uncooked buckwheat groats

1 ½ teaspoons oregano

1 teaspoon onion powder

1 teaspoon thyme

½ cup diced sweet onion

½ cup diced celery

6 large cloves garlic, minced (about ¼ cup)

½ cup coconut flour or gluten-free oat flour for coating sides of burgers

1. Preheat the oven to 400°F. Line a baking sheet with parchment paper.

2. Peel the squash, remove the seeds, and cut the squash into ½-inch cubes. Place the squash in a large bowl with 1 tablespoon olive oil and ½ teaspoon each of salt, paprika, and chile powder. Mix well with your hands until coated. Spread the squash on a baking sheet in a single layer and bake for 30 minutes, turning the squash after 15 minutes. Remove from the oven and set aside to cool. If baking the burgers, reduce the oven temperture to 375°F.

3. While the squash is roasting, combine the buckwheat groats and 2 cups water in a medium saucepan. Bring to a boil, cover, and reduce the heat to a simmer. Cook 7 to 10 minutes until the water has been absorbed and the groats are tender. Remove from the heat and set aside.

4. In a small bowl combine the oregano, 1 teaspoon paprika, onion powder, 1 teaspoon chile powder, 1 teaspoon salt, and thyme and mix well.

5. Place 1 tablespoon olive oil in a medium frying pan over medium heat. When heated, add the onion, celery, and garlic. Stir and add half of the seasoning

mix, about 1 tablespoon. Sauté until the onion starts to become soft and translucent, about 5 minutes. When done, remove from the heat.

6. Place the roasted squash in a food processor and pulse until mostly smooth. There should be no liquid. Alternatively, you can mash it by hand Add the squash and 2½ cups cooked buckwheat to a medium mixing bowl. Stir with a wooden spoon to combine. Add the veggie and spice sauté to the bowl and stir to combine. Add the remaining half of spice mix to the burger mixture and stir to combine well.

7. Place the coconut flour or oat flour in a small shallow bowl or plate. To make the burger patties, use ⅓ cup of burger mixture for each patty. Form into a tightly packed ball in your hand and flatten between your palms, about 3 inches in diameter and ½-inch thick. Place the burger on the flour and gently brush off the extra flour. Repeat on the opposite side.

8. Cook the burgers. To fry them, heat about 1 teaspoon of olive oil in a nonstick frying pan over medium heat. Place the burgers in the pan when the oil is hot. Cook 5 to 7 minutes on each side until the patties are firm and beginning to brown.

9. If baking, place the burgers on a parchment-lined baking sheet and bake at 375°F for 15 minutes on each side.

Serving, Storing, and Reheating

Serving options: Eat as a traditional burger, served on top of a salad or plated with your favorite veggie side dish.

Storage: The leftovers keep well in the refrigerator in a sealed container for 3 to 5 days. You can freeze them by wrapping them individually in wax paper and placing them into a zip-top bag in the freezer. Remove from the freezer several hours before reheating to allow time to thaw.

Reheating: Heat a nonstick pan over medium heat. Place the burgers in the pan and warm for 2 to 3 minutes on each side.

Vegan Zucchini Lasagna

Makes 12 slices

When I was a kid, if I found out we were having homemade lasagna for dinner I would look forward to it all day—as well as the leftovers the next day. This lasagna has been a lifesaver for those moments when I crave my favorite decadent comfort food. The zucchini has just the right texture to replace noodles, and the creamy herbed ricotta pairs well with a robust marinara, transforming nontraditional ingredients into an Italian classic. This recipe is prep-ahead friendly and reheats easily to make great leftovers—if there are any!

Prep time: 40 minutes (includes time for weeping zucchini; does not include time for making sauce and cheeses, if not using store-bought)   **Cook time:** 40 minutes

3 or 4 medium zucchini

salt, for weeping zucchini

2 ½ cups Easy Marinara Sauce
(page 185) or store-bought

2 cups Vegan Ricotta Cheese
(page 81) or store-bought

1 cup shredded vegan mozzarella

¼ cup Vegan Parmesan Cheese
(page 83) or store-bought

1. Preheat the oven to 350°F. If the sauce, ricotta, and Parmesan cheeses were prepared in advance, remove the items from the refrigerator and allow them to come to room temperature, about 1 hour. If using store-bought ricotta, gently stir in the herb seasoning (see tip).

2. Remove the ends of the zucchini and slice lengthwise in roughly 18 one-eighth-inch-thick slices. I like to cut the 6 slices for the top layer slightly thinner.

(continued on page 183)

NOTES

- Precooked gluten-free lasagna noodles may be substituted for zucchini in this recipe.

Quick prep: Prepared ingredients may be used for the marinara sauce and vegan cheeses.

Prep ahead: Easy Marinara Sauce (page 185), Vegan Ricotta Cheese (page 81), and Vegan Parmesan (page 83) can be made in advance and refrigerated for 1 to 2 days until ready to assemble lasagna.

Meal Prep Game Plan: If preparing this dish on the same day and using my recipes for Vegan Ricotta Cheese and Vegan Parmesan, allow time to soak the nuts. I recommend soaking the nuts and then preparing the sauce. While the sauce simmers make the ricotta and Parmesan cheeses. Last, weep the zucchini.

3. Place a cooling rack on a baking sheet with sides. Lay the zucchini slices flat in one layer on the cooling rack and sprinkle with salt on each side. Allow to weep for 30 minutes. Alternatively, you may place the zucchini in a strainer in your sink, salt it, and allow it to weep for 30 minutes.

4. After 30 minutes, rinse the salt from the zucchini and place the slices flat on a paper towel. Place a second paper towel on top and lightly blot off the excess water.

5. Spread a thin layer of sauce, about ½ cup, on the bottom of a 12 x 7½-inch glass casserole pan (a 13 x 9-inch pan will work with a little extra of all the ingredients). Place a single layer of zucchini slices, about 6 slices, across the bottom of the pan parallel to the short side of the pan. Place a dollop of ricotta on each slice and spread evenly, using about 1 cup for the whole layer. Sprinkle with ½ cup of mozzarella cheese and then top with ¾ cup sauce. Repeat this process for a second layer.

6. After completing the second lasagna layer, top the casserole with a third layer of zucchini. Spread with another layer of sauce, about ½ cup, and sprinkle with about ¼ cup of Parmesan or mozzarella.

7. Cover the pan with foil and bake for about 40 minutes, removing the foil after 20 minutes. Allow more or less cooking time, depending on thickness of sauce. Remove from the oven and cool for at least 10 minutes before serving to allow for the lasagna to set. Store in the refrigerator in a covered dish for 2 to 3 days.

Tip: If using ready-made vegan ricotta, add 1½ teaspoons dried oregano, 1½ teaspoons finely ground sea salt (less if store-bought cheese tastes salty), 1 teaspoon dried basil, ¼ teaspoon garlic powder, and a pinch black pepper for a beautiful herb blend.

Easy Marinara Sauce

Makes 6 cups

This is my go-to sauce for a plate of pasta. It's a great make-ahead staple to have in the freezer for a quick thaw. It is also delicious as a component of a dish such as Vegan Zucchini Lasagna (page 181).

Prep time: 10 minutes   **Cook time:** 1 hour

1 tablespoon olive oil, or vegetable broth or water for an oil-free option (page 17)

1 medium onion, chopped

5 large cloves garlic, minced (more or less to taste)

¼ cup minced fresh parsley or 2 tablespoons dried parsley

2 tablespoons minced fresh basil or 1 tablespoon dried basil

1 teaspoon dried oregano

1 teaspoon finely ground sea salt, plus more to taste

¼ teaspoon finely ground black pepper, plus more to taste

1 (28-ounce) can tomato puree, about 3 ¼ cups

1 (29-ounce) can tomato sauce, about 3 ¼ cups

chile powder (optional)

1. Heat the olive oil, broth, or water in a 4-quart wide-bottom saucepan over medium heat. Add the onion and garlic and sauté until golden, about 3 to 5 minutes. Add the parsley, basil, oregano, salt, and black pepper. Stir together and sauté for an additional minute.

2. Add the tomato puree and sauce to the mixture and stir well. Taste and add any additional dry seasonings such as granulated garlic, basil, parsley, or chile powder in very small increments (¼ teaspoon), if desired. Keep in mind, the seasonings will intensify once cooked. I like to add a little chile powder at this point as it brings a hint of umami to the sauce.

3. Bring the sauce to a rapid boil and continue boiling for 8 to 10 minutes. Reduce the heat and simmer for 50 minutes, stirring periodically.

4. Serve over pasta and enjoy. If storing, let the sauce cool and then place in an airtight glass container in the refrigerator for 5 days or freeze for 1 to 2 months.

Ratatouille and Beans

Makes 5 one-cup servings

After fine-tuning just the right balance of seasonings and fresh vegetables, I selected the perfect legumes—cannellini beans and chickpeas—to add to this expressive medley. It is a vibrant dish that will bring a splash of color to your dinner and leave you feeling satisfied and nourished.

Prep time: 15 minutes (including skinning tomatoes)   **Cook time:** 30 minutes

1 cup vegetable broth, divided

6 large cloves garlic, minced, about 3 to 4 tablespoons

1 small onion, diced, about ½ cup

1 stalk celery, diced, about ⅓ cup

¾ teaspoon finely ground sea salt

½ teaspoon oregano

⅛ teaspoon cayenne pepper

dash finely ground black pepper

½ red bell pepper, diced, about ½ cup

1 medium carrot, diced, about ¼ cup

1 medium zucchini, chopped in ½-inch pieces, about 2 cups

5 skinned tomatoes (see page 19) or 3 cups canned tomatoes, chopped

1 cup cannellini beans or other white bean, lightly rinsed

¼ cup chickpeas, lightly rinsed (optional)

1. Using a large, deep sauté pan with at least 3-inch sides, a saucepan, or a Dutch oven, warm ¼ cup vegetable broth and sauté the garlic and onion until translucent, about 3 minutes. Alternatively, 1 teaspoon of olive oil may be used instead of the vegetable broth for sautéing, but the dish will no longer be oil-free.

2. Add the celery, salt, oregano, cayenne, and black pepper. Stir to combine and sauté until the celery is translucent, about 2 minutes.

3. Add the red bell pepper, carrot, and zucchini. Sauté 3 minutes, stirring occasionally. Add the chopped tomato and bring to a boil. Reduce heat to a simmer, about 5 minutes. Taste and add additional seasoning, if desired.

4. Add the beans or beans and chickpeas and ¼ to ½ cup broth. More or less broth may be added according to the desired amount of liquid. Stir together and continue cooking until the beans are warm, about 2 to 3 minutes.

5. Serve in a bowl as a stew or over pasta. Store in a glass container in the refrigerator for 4 to 5 days. Reheat on the stovetop over medium-low heat. Additional broth may be added 1 tablespoon at a time if the ratatouille has thickened.

Thai Basil Alfredo

Makes 3 cups (enough to dress 1 pound of pasta)

When you're craving something decadent and filling, look no farther. This velvety and ultra-creamy sauce is an opulent, dairy-free version of an Italian favorite. The addition of Thai basil, roasted garlic, and green onions brings a gentle earthiness that enhances the rich base. Traditionally, this sauce would be served over fettuccine, but the sauce can be used with most types of pasta. Baby Arugula and Corn Salad (page 65) makes a wonderful complement to this dish.

Prep time: 5 minutes   **Cook time:** 30 minutes

1 pound gluten-free pasta

2 cups raw cashews, soaked

Roasted Garlic (see page 19)

¾ cup unsweetened plant-based milk (an additional ¼ cup may be used to thin sauce, if necessary)

2 tablespoons plus 1 teaspoon lemon juice

1 tablespoon green onion, chopped (use the white part)

2 to 3 teaspoons nutritional yeast flakes, to taste

1 teaspoon finely ground sea salt (an additional ½ teaspoon may be added, to taste)

8 to 10 leaves Thai basil, chopped

dash finely ground black pepper

> **NOTES**
> – Soaking cashews is required prior to starting this recipe. See page 17 for quick-soak or overnight-soak instructions. If using the quick-soak method, let cashews soak for 40 minutes.
>
> **Oil-free:** To make this recipe oil-free, simply omit the oil when roasting the garlic.
>
> **Cook Time:** The only cooking required for this dish is roasting the garlic and cooking the pasta.
>
> **Basil:** Thai basil is usually found in the fresh herb section of your grocery store. Fresh basil can be substituted but use only 4 to 5 leaves.

1. Prepare the pasta according to the package instructions.

2. While the pasta cooks, prepare the sauce. Place the soaked cashews, 8 to 10 cloves of roasted garlic, and the remaining ingredients in a blender. Pulse a few times to break the cashews into smaller pieces then blend at high speed until smooth. Pause when necessary to scrape down the sides of the container.

Once the sauce is smooth and creamy, taste and add more nutritional yeast and/or salt and pepper to suit your personal preference. If the sauce is too thick, additional plant-based milk may be added and blended in 1 tablespoon at a time, not to exceed ¼ cup.

3. Serve the sauce over warm pasta. The sauce may be refrigerated in an airtight container for at least 1 week. Reheat in a saucepan over low heat, stirring frequently. If the sauce is too thick. a small amount of plant-based milk may be added 1 tablespoon at a time, not to exceed ¼ cup.

Turmeric Cauliflower and Lentils over Baked Potato

Makes 6 one-cup servings

What do you get when you combine a healthfully seasoned vegetable, a satisfying plant-based protein, and a comforting starch? One seriously gratifying meal! This comforting entrée fills your belly while boasting all of the antioxidant and anti-inflammatory benefits of turmeric. But healthy benefits aside, I eat this dish with regularity because it tastes so good!

Prep time: 10 minutes   **Cook time**: 45 minutes

4 to 6 baking potatoes

1 teaspoon olive oil plus more for coating potatoes, or 3 to 4 tablespoons vegetable broth or water for an oil-free option (page 17)

¾ cup slivered almonds, divided (omit for nut-free version)

½ cup onion, diced

3 cloves garlic, minced

1 head cauliflower, chopped into 1-inch pieces, about 5 to 6 cups

1 to 2 teaspoons ground turmeric, to taste

½ teaspoon cumin

½ teaspoon red pepper flakes

½ teaspoon finely ground sea salt, plus more for baking potato

½ teaspoon finely ground black pepper

3 ½ cups vegetable broth

(continued on the following page)

1. Preheat the oven to 425°F. Wash and dry the potatoes. Pierce each potato with a fork 2 to 3 times. Rub oil on the potato skin (omit for an oil-free option) and sprinkle with salt. Place the potatoes on a baking sheet and bake for about 45 minutes, turning over halfway through. Potatoes are done when fork-tender. One minute prior to removing the tray from the oven, scatter half of the almond slivers on the tray around the potatoes to brown. Remove the tray from the oven and place on a cooling rack.

2. Heat the olive oil or vegetable broth in a large skillet or Dutch oven over medium heat. Add the onion and garlic and sauté until the onion begins to turn translucent, about 3 minutes. Add the cauliflower and continue to sauté until golden brown, about 8 minutes. Add the turmeric, cumin, red pepper flakes, salt, and pepper. Combine well and continue sautéing for an additional 2 minutes.

3. Add the vegetable broth to the pan with the cauliflower mixture and gently scrape the bottom of the pan to deglaze. Add the lentils, bring the broth to a boil, and reduce to a simmer for 15 minutes.

1 cup red lentils, rinsed and drained

1 tablespoon lemon juice or red wine vinegar

2 tablespoons green onions, chopped, plus more for garnish

4. After 15 minutes, add the lemon juice or vinegar, green onions, and untoasted almond slivers to the pan and stir to combine.

5. To serve, slice open the baked potatoes lengthwise. Use a fork to fluff and loosen the potato. A drizzle of olive oil may be added to the potato (skip for an oil-free option). Then spoon about ½ cup of the turmeric cauliflower and lentils on top of the potato and serve.

6. Store leftover potatoes for about 1 day and leftover cauliflower lentils for about 3 to 4 days in an airtight container in the refrigerator. To reheat the baked potato, wrap in foil and place in a standard oven or toaster oven for 20 minutes at 350°F. The cauliflower lentils can be reheated in a saucepan over low heat and served over leftover baked potato or in a bowl as a side dish.

Curried Chickpeas, Asparagus, and Cauliflower

Servings: 5

The secret to this curry dish is to make a slurry of creamy plant-based milk and tapioca starch. It makes a zippy rich dinner, perfect for when you are longing for a change of pace in your plant-based lineup. I suggest serving it over made-ahead rice.

Prep time: 5 minutes   **Cook time:** 20 minutes

1 teaspoon olive oil, or 3 to 4 tablespoons vegetable broth or water for an oil-free option (page 17)

½ head cauliflower cut into small florets, about 4 cups

3 teaspoons granulated garlic, divided

3 teaspoons curry powder, divided

1½ teaspoons finely ground sea salt, divided

1 teaspoon ginger

1 teaspoon paprika, divided

1 bunch asparagus cut into 1-inch lengths, about 3 cups

1 (15-ounce) can chickpeas, drained

1 cup unsweetened plant-based milk (I use cashew but this is not nut-free)

1 tablespoon tapioca starch/ flour

⅓ cup chopped green onions, about 2 stalks

1. Heat the oil or broth in a large skillet over medium/high heat. Add the cauliflower to the pan and season with 2 teaspoons granulated garlic, 2 teaspoons curry powder, 1 teaspoon salt, ginger, and ¾ teaspoon paprika. Stir to evenly coat the cauliflower with the seasoning. Sauté until the cauliflower begins to turn tender, about 7 to 8 minutes, stirring occasionally. If you are not using a nonstick pan some of the spices may stick to the bottom. They will easily scrape off in step 4.

2. Move the cauliflower to the perimeter of the pan and add the asparagus to the center. Season the asparagus with 1 teaspoon granulated garlic, 1 teaspoon curry powder, ½ teaspoon salt, and ¼ teaspoon paprika. Stir and sauté until tender, about 7 to 8 minutes.

3. Mix the cauliflower and asparagus together and move to the perimeter of the pan. Add the chickpeas to the center and sauté until warm, about 3 minutes.

4. In a small bowl whisk together the plant-based milk and tapioca starch. Stir together the cauliflower, asparagus, and chickpeas and move to the perimeter

of the pan. Add the slurry to the center of the pan and stir for about 1 minute until it begins to thicken. If you are not using a nonstick pan, lightly scrape the bottom to loosen any remaining spices. Once the liquid begins to thicken, about 2 to 3 minutes, mix in the vegetables from the perimeter. Stir in the green onions, reserving some for a garnish. Serve immediately. If desired, serve this dish over a bed of rice. Leftovers may be stored in an airtight container in the refrigerator for 2 to 3 days and reheated on the stovetop over low heat for 8 to 10 minutes, stirring occasionally.

Buckwheat Bolognese

Servings: 6

Traditional Bolognese uses ground beef or pork to flavor a basic red sauce. In this hearty plant-based version I used buckwheat, as it offers an umami flavor and a texture that generously fills out the sauce. Serve it over pasta or zoodles.

Prep time: 10 minutes   **Cook time:** 25 minutes

1 ½ teaspoons olive oil, or vegetable broth or water for an oil-free option (see page 17), divided

³⁄₄ cup diced sweet onion, divided

¹⁄₃ cup diced green bell pepper

1 tablespoon minced fresh garlic

¹⁄₂ teaspoon finely ground sea salt, divided

1 cup uncooked buckwheat groats, rinsed and drained

2 cups vegetable broth

2 (15-ounce) cans tomato sauce

2 tablespoons minced fresh basil, about 15 medium leaves or 2 teaspoons dried basil

³⁄₄ teaspoon dried oregano

¹⁄₂ teaspoon granulated garlic

1. Heat 1 teaspoon oil in a medium saucepan over medium heat. Sauté ½ cup onion, green pepper, garlic, and ¼ teaspoon salt until the onion is translucent, about 5 minutes.

2. Add the buckwheat groats to the saucepan and stir for 1 to 2 minutes to lightly brown some of the buckwheat. Then add the vegetable broth to the saucepan and bring to a boil. Cover, reduce to a simmer, and cook until the buckwheat is tender, about 10 minutes. Cover and set aside.

3. While the buckwheat is cooking, warm ½ teaspoon oil in a large skillet over medium heat. Add the remaining onion and salt. Sauté until the onion becomes translucent, about 3 minutes. Stir in the tomato sauce, and add the basil, oregano, and granulated garlic. Stir to combine and bring the sauce to a simmer, stirring periodically. Continue to cook for about 10 minutes, stirring occasionally. After 10 minutes, mix in 2 to 3 cups of the buckwheat mixture, depending on desired thickness. Serve the sauce over pasta or zoodles. Leftovers may be refrigerated for 3 to 5 days and reheated on the stovetop over low heat for about 10 to 15 minutes, stirring occasionally.

Avocado Pesto over Zoodles

Servings: 8 (recipe makes about 1 cup of sauce)

When you need a satisfying but healthy way to enjoy your dinner after a long day, whip up this easy dish. The buttery taste of avocado softens the intensity of the fresh herbs in this quick dish. The avocado's natural fat also helps the pesto adhere to my favorite pasta alternative—zoodles.

Prep time: 5 minutes   **Cook time:** none

1 large ripe avocado, peeled
and sliced (about 1 ½ cups
chopped)

1 cup fresh basil, loosely packed

½ cup pine nuts

2 tablespoons lemon juice

1 clove garlic, minced

½ teaspoon sea salt, to taste

dash finely ground black pepper

3 to 4 medium zucchinis

Pine nuts or Vegan Parmesan
Cheese (page 83) for topping

1. Make the Avocado Pesto. Place the avocado, basil, pine nuts, lemon juice, garlic, salt, and pepper in a food processor or high-speed blender. Pulse a few times to break down the ingredients and then process until creamy. Taste the sauce and, if needed, add more lemon juice, garlic, or salt and pepper to taste. Set aside.

2. Using a spiralizer, prepare the zucchini. Place the zoodles on a paper towel to absorb any water that may weep from the squash. Place the zoodles in a large bowl.

3. If serving at room temperature, gently toss the zoodles in the sauce. If serving warmed, add the zoodles and sauce to a medium skillet over low heat to warm, about 2 to 3 minutes. When ready to serve, top with pine nuts or Vegan Parmesan Cheese, if desired.

Tip: This sauce can also be served with 1 pound of gluten-free pasta.

Tangy Mushroom Stroganoff

Servings: 4

With just a half hour of time and effort, you will be eating a rich dish that satisfies just like the original recipe developed in mid-nineteenth century Russia. No meat or cream required!

Prep time: 10 minutes   **Cook time:** 20 minutes

¾ cup cashews, soaked

1 cup cashew milk, or other mild-tasting plant-based milk

8 ounces gluten-free pasta

1 teaspoon olive oil

1 medium diced sweet onion, about 1 cup

2 tablespoons minced garlic

¾ teaspoon finely ground sea salt, divided

8 ounces (about 20 medium) cremini mushrooms, cleaned (see page 201) and thinly sliced

1 teaspoon dried thyme

¼ cup white wine vinegar

2 tablespoons coconut aminos or gluten-free soy sauce (for a non–soy free option)

dash black pepper, to taste

> **NOTE**
> – Soaking cashews is required prior to starting this recipe. See page 17 for quick-soak or overnight-soak instructions.

1. Place the cashews and cashew milk in a blender. Pulse a few times to break up the cashews, then blend on high speed until smooth, about 3 to 5 minutes. Be sure to pause periodically to scrape down the sides. Leave covered and set aside.

2. Prepare the pasta according to the directions on the package and set aside.

3. Heat the oil in a medium or large skillet over medium heat. Add the onion, garlic, and ¼ teaspoon salt to the pan and sauté until the onion just begins to turn translucent, about 3 to 5 minutes. Push the onion and garlic to the side of the pan and add the sliced mushrooms and thyme to the center. Cook until the mushrooms are lightly browned, about 5 minutes. Combine the mushrooms with the onion and garlic and cook for an additional minute.

4. Add the vinegar, coconut aminos, remaining salt, and a dash of black pepper. Stir to combine and increase the heat to high. Stirring frequently, let the liquid reduce, about 5 minutes.

5. Reduce the heat back to medium. Pour in the cashew cream. Stir until well combined and let it thicken for about 4 to 5 minutes, stirring frequently. If the sauce becomes too thick, add additional cashew milk 1 tablespoon at a time, not to exceed 3 tablespoons, and stir. Taste and add salt or pepper, if desired. Serve immediately over pasta. Store any leftovers in an airtight container in the refrigerator for 2 to 3 days. Reheat on the stovetop over medium-low heat, and add cashew milk to thin the sauce, if necessary.

Portobello Steak with Tomato-Caper Sauce

Servings: 4

There are times when you want a dinner that requires a knife and fork, for the kind of hunger that makes you want to *feel full*. These portobello steaks provide that satisfying chew while being tender enough to feel like a melt-in-your-mouth entrée. Top the portobello with a zesty tomato sauce featuring capers, garlic, and olives, and you've got a meal of substance and nourishment.

Prep time: 10 minutes **Cook time:** 20 minutes

¼ cup red wine vinegar

2 tablespoons coconut aminos or gluten-free soy sauce (for a non—soy free option)

1 tablespoon prepared mustard

½ teaspoon granulated garlic

½ teaspoon onion powder

½ teaspoon sea salt

4 portobello mushrooms, stems and gills removed and scrubbed clean

2 teaspoons olive oil, or vegetable broth or water for an oil-free option (page 17)

2 tablespoons minced garlic

2 tablespoons nonpareil capers

½ cup sliced olives (I use a mix of Kalamata, Spanish, and Castelvetrano)

1 (15-ounce) can tomato sauce

sea salt and black pepper, to taste

fresh parsley for garnish, if desired

> **NOTE**
> – Prep time does not include marinating the mushrooms. They will need 1 hour to marinate before cooking this dish.

1. In a small bowl, whisk together the red wine vinegar, coconut aminos, mustard, garlic, onion powder, and salt.

2. Pour the marinade in a resealable plastic bag. Place the portobellos one at a time in the bag, seal the bag, and toss to coat the mushrooms thoroughly. Place them top down in a glass pan. Pour the remaining marinade from the bag over the mushrooms and cover. Refrigerate and marinate 1 hour.

3. Heat 1 teaspoon olive oil in a medium or large skillet on medium-high heat. Add the minced garlic and capers and sauté for 4 to 5 minutes until the garlic is golden brown. Gently stir with a large spatula. Add the sliced olives, stir, and sauté for 1 minute. Add the tomato sauce and gently stir with a spatula. Continue cooking for 15 minutes at a low simmer, while stirring periodically. Remove from the heat and set aside.

How to Clean Mushrooms

There is some debate over how to clean mushrooms. Some people say to wipe them with a paper towel and never use water. I belong to the school of thought that wants to minimize the amount of dirt and harmful impurities. You can dunk, not soak, the mushrooms in a bowl of **6 cups water** and ⅓ **cup distilled white vinegar solution**, massage the dirt off the mushrooms while they are submerged, then rinse and wipe dry with a paper towel. No mushy mushrooms and—I hope—no impurities.

4. While the sauce simmers, cook the mushrooms. Remove the portobellos from the marinade and place on a plate top side down. Season with salt and pepper.

5. Add 1 teaspoon olive oil or a couple of tablespoons of the remaining marinade to a medium or large skillet over medium-high heat. Once hot, place the portobello caps top side up in the pan. Season the tops with salt and pepper. Cook for 3 to 4 minutes on each side (more time is required for larger portobellos). They should be nicely browned and tender. Alternatively, they can be cooked on a grill over medium heat. The cooking time should remain the same.

6. Remove the portobello steaks from the pan with tongs and gently pour off any liquid that may have seeped from the mushrooms. Place the portobello steaks on a plate and spoon the tomato-caper sauce on top. Sprinkle with fresh parsley, if desired. Serve immediately.

Pasta e Fagioli

Servings: 6

The quintessential Italian comfort soup, this dish's name literally translates to "pasta and beans." Add potato, and now you've got a dish to warm you on the coldest of days. Many variations exist of this dish, from a soup-like structure to a thick, hearty stew you can practically eat with a fork. My version has a thicker base to support the potato and beans, but still has enough starchy broth that you will want a spoon to get every last drop.

Prep time: 5 minutes   **Cook time:** 40 minutes

1 teaspoon olive oil, or vegetable broth or water for an oil-free option (page 17)

1 medium sweet onion, diced, about 1 cup

2 carrots, peeled and diced

1 stalk celery, diced

2 tablespoons minced garlic

¾ teaspoon finely ground sea salt, divided

⅛ teaspoon red pepper flakes (optional)

1 medium potato, peeled and diced, about 1 cup

30 ounces crushed tomatoes in puree, **or** 15 ounces tomato sauce plus 15 ounces diced tomatoes

1 cup vegetable broth

1 (15-ounce) can Great Northern beans, rinsed and drained (other mild white bean like cannellini may be substituted)

1 teaspoon dried oregano

(continued on the following page)

1. Heat 1 teaspoon oil in a stockpot or Dutch oven over medium heat. Sauté the onion, carrot, celery, garlic, ¼ teaspoon salt, and red pepper flakes, if desired, until the onion is translucent, about 5 minutes. Add the potato, stir to combine, and cook for an additional 3 to 5 minutes.

2. Add the tomatoes, vegetable broth, beans, oregano, thyme, and remaining salt and black pepper, to taste. Stir together and bring to a boil. Reduce the heat to a simmer, cover, and cook for about 10 minutes or until the potato is tender.

3. Add the pasta to the pot and stir to combine. Cook for 15 to 20 minutes, until the pasta and potatoes are tender. If a thinner consistency is desired, add an additional ¼ cup vegetable broth. Ladle into a bowl and serve immediately. Store in an airtight container in the refrigerator for 3 to 5 days. Leftovers may be reheated over low heat. Add water or vegetable broth by the tablespoon if thinning is necessary.

³/₄ teaspoon dried thyme

black pepper, to taste

1 cup uncooked gluten-free pasta (I use brown rice fusilli pasta)

Variation

Don't want to add potatoes or don't have them on-hand? Substitute an additional 15-ounce can of beans instead.

Broccoli Asparagus Apple Risotto

Servings: 4

Each bite of this creamy risotto offers an array of subtle notes like a complex wine, and the tastes and textures are sure to please. This dish will be equally enjoyed served to dinner guests or eaten out of a bowl on the couch as you watch your favorite movie.

Prep time: 10 minutes   **Cook time:** 40 minutes

1 teaspoon olive oil, or vegetable broth or water for an oil-free option (page 17)

1 cup leek, sliced into ⅛-inch half moons, white part only

1 ¼ cups asparagus, trimmed and sliced into 1-inch pieces

2 cups broccolini or young broccoli, trimmed and sliced into 1-inch pieces

1 teaspoon dried thyme

½ teaspoon finely ground sea salt, divided

¼ teaspoon coarsely ground black pepper

⅛ teaspoon granulated garlic

1 large sweet apple, peeled, cored, and diced

1 cup uncooked Arborio rice

4 cups vegetable broth

1. Add the olive oil to a medium or large skillet and place over medium heat. Add the leeks, asparagus, broccoli, thyme, ¼ teaspoon salt, pepper, and granulated garlic and sauté for 4 to 5 minutes. Remove the vegetables from the pan and place on a large plate in a single layer. The vegetables should still be bright green and crunchy as they will continue to cook after being removed from the pan. Set aside.

2. Add the apple to the pan, season with the remaining ¼ teaspoon salt, and sauté until golden and tender, about 10 minutes.

3. Add the Arborio rice to the skillet and combine with the apple. Stir continuously until the rice begins to turn translucent, about 5 minutes. Add 1 cup of broth to the skillet and stir continuously until all of the stock has been absorbed by the rice. Add the remaining broth in 1 cup increments, stirring and allowing the broth to be absorbed before adding the next cup.

4. Once all the broth has been added and is absorbed, return the vegetables to the pan and gently stir to combine. Reduce the heat to medium-low and continue to gently stir until the vegetables have warmed, about 1 to 2 minutes. Taste and adjust salt and pepper, if desired. Serve immediately.

Veggie Subs

Servings: 4

Sometimes you're just craving a big old sub. Before I adopted a plant-based diet, I would get those cravings. But as the years passed, I noticed I was having the sub shops add less meat and more and more veggies. Lettuce, tomatoes, onions, pickles, peppers, olives—before long, the sandwich was 95 percent vegetables; removing the meat had no impact whatsoever. Still one of my favorite comfort-style foods, I whip up this specific veggie sub recipe when I want to seriously chow down.

Prep time: 5 minutes   **Cook time:** 10 minutes

1 teaspoon olive oil, or vegetable broth or water for an oil-free option (page 17)

½ cup green olives with pimento, chopped, about 12 medium olives

2 medium green onions, chopped, about ⅓ cup

1 to 1½ tablespoons minced garlic

1½ to 2 teaspoons nonpareil capers, about 25

4 medium stalks broccolini or young broccoli, stems and florets cut into 1-inch pieces

1¼ cups chopped green, yellow, orange, or red bell pepper

1 cup shaved carrot

⅛ teaspoon dried thyme, to taste

salt and pepper, to taste

4 gluten-free hoagies, submarine-style rolls, Kaiser rolls, or baguettes

1. Heat 1 teaspoon oil in a medium or large skillet over medium heat. Sauté the olives, green onions, garlic, and capers until fragrant, about 3 minutes. Push to the perimeter of the pan and add the broccolini to the middle of the pan. Sauté for about 3 minutes.

2. Add the bell pepper, carrot, thyme, salt, and pepper to the pan, and sauté for about 2 minutes. Gently fold in the ingredients from the perimeter of the pan and add additional seasoning, if desired.

3. Toast the rolls, if desired. Coat with the plant-based mayo, Ranch Dressing, or a smashed ripe avocado. Top the rolls with the vegetables and serve immediately.

(continued on the following page)

plant-based mayo, for serving

Ranch Dressing (page 73), for serving

smashed ripe Hass avocado, for serving

Tip: If you can't find broccolini or young broccoli, mature or large stalks will do. Just peel the stem first as this will make it more tender.

Go Bold or Go Home Chili

Servings: 6

The secret ingredient to making this recipe taste just like old school chili is lentils. *Exploded* lentils. If you cook them too hard, they pop open and soften and act as a thickening agent with a result similar to stew. The balance between the starchy insides of the lentils and the juicy diced tomatoes creates a chili so thick and authentic your omnivore guests will have eaten half a bowl before they realize the dish is meatless.

Prep time: 10 minutes   **Cook time:** 55 minutes

1 cup dried red lentils, rinsed

1 medium onion, diced

1 medium green bell pepper, diced, about ½ cup

⅓ cup diced celery

1 to 2 tablespoons minced garlic

1 ½ teaspoons finely ground sea salt, divided

3 tablespoons chile powder

2 teaspoons cumin

1 teaspoon paprika

½ teaspoon finely ground black pepper

dash red pepper flakes (optional)

1 (28-ounce) can diced tomatoes in juice

1 (15-ounce) can red beans or kidney beans, rinsed and drained

> NOTE
> – Red lentils are more delicate than their green or brown counterparts. Customarily, they are cooked at a very gentle simmer. For this recipe, I cook the lentils at an active simmer which causes their fragile skins to rupture and free the starchy inside. This allows them to act as a thickening agent for the chili and adds an authentic texture too.

1. Place the dried lentils in a strainer and rinse with cold water. Transfer to a saucepan and add 3 cups filtered water, cover, and bring to a boil. Uncover the pan, reduce the heat to medium-low, and simmer for about 20 to 25 minutes or until tender and the water is absorbed. The lentils will become quite mushy, almost like a thick stew.

2. Shortly before the lentils are finished cooking, place a 6-quart saucepan over medium-high heat. Add the onion, green bell pepper, celery, garlic, and ¼ teaspoon salt. Sauté until the onion becomes translucent, about

5 minutes. The salt will help the vegetables release water, so no oil or extra water is required at this time.

3. Add ¼ cup water to the pan and stir to deglaze. Add the lentils to the pan and stir to combine. Add the chile powder, cumin, the remaining salt, paprika, black pepper, and red pepper flakes, if desired. Combine the seasonings with the ingredients and cook for 1 to 2 minutes.

4. Add the tomatoes and their juice and the beans to the pot, stir, and reduce heat to low. Simmer for about 30 minutes, stirring occasionally. After 30 minutes, check the seasonings and adjust to taste and serve. If you want a thicker stew, a longer simmer will result in a richer, thicker, concentrated chili.

5. Store in an airtight glass container in the refrigerator for 5 to 7 days. Reheat over medium-low heat. Add water, 1 tablespoon at a time, if thinning is necessary.

Crabless Cakes

Servings: eight 2 1/2-inch cakes

I was born and raised in Maryland, and if my home state is known for one dish, it is without question the crab cake—a subtle, tender seafood patty that is pan-fried and seasoned with a unique blend known as Old Bay. As much about texture as it is taste, the recipe has become one of the most coveted dishes on the central East Coast. By replacing the crabmeat with torn hearts of palm, the look, texture, taste, and buttery softness are better than the original. This version is healthier too—baked rather than pan-fried.

Prep time: 10 minutes   **Cook time:** 18 minutes

1 (14- to 15-ounce) can hearts of palm, rinsed and drained

1/4 cup vegan mayonnaise

1 teaspoon Old Bay or other seafood seasoning

1 teaspoon prepared mustard

1/2 teaspoon coconut aminos or vegan Worcestershire

1/2 teaspoon finely ground sea salt

1/8 teaspoon freshly cracked black pepper

1/4 cup finely chopped green onions, about 1 stalk

1/2 cup gluten-free panko or very fine bread crumbs, divided

cocktail sauce, for serving

1. Preheat the oven to 400°F. Line a baking sheet with parchment paper.

2. Thinly slice the hearts of palm lengthwise. Cut the slices into ¾-inch pieces. Using your fingers, gently pull any larger pieces into shreds.

3. In a medium bowl, whisk together the mayonnaise, Old Bay, mustard, coconut aminos, salt, and pepper until well blended. Stir in the hearts of palm and green onions until well combined.

4. Add ⅓ cup of the bread crumbs to the hearts of palm mixture and gently mix in. Form eight patties, 2 tablespoons each.

5. Add the remaining bread crumbs to a small dish. Dredge both sides of the patties in bread crumbs, pressing gently to adhere. Place on the baking sheet, evenly spaced.

6. Bake for 18 minutes until the cakes are light golden brown, flipping over after 13 minutes. Remove them from the oven and serve immediately with your favorite cocktail sauce. Leftovers will keep well in the refrigerator for 2 to 3 days.

CHAPTER 10

Desserts
and
Indulgences

Chocolate Chickpea Bark

Makes 10 to 12 pieces

This indulgent treat delivers a complete taste and texture experience: sweet and salty to soft and crunchy. If you lament giving up chocolate-covered pretzels after going gluten-free, this snack will seem heaven-sent. And thanks to the chickpeas, you'll get a generous helping of plant-based protein. Kids and grown-ups alike will be hooked from the very first bite! A double batch is standard in our household.

Prep time: 10 minutes   **Cook time:** 40 minutes

1 (15-ounce) can chickpeas, rinsed and drained

1 tablespoon olive oil

¼ teaspoon finely ground sea salt

1 cup vegan semi-sweet chocolate chips

> **NOTE**
> – Refrigeration is required for 2 to 3 hours before serving.

1. Preheat the oven to 400°F. Line a baking sheet with parchment paper.

2. Pour the chickpeas into a strainer and rinse with cool water. Shake off the excess water and spread the chickpeas onto a tea towel. Gently rub them with the towel in a circular motion. Discard any skins that fall off.

3. Place the chickpeas on the baking sheet and allow them to dry to the touch. It is important that the chickpeas dry completely before coating them in oil or they will not become crunchy when roasted. To shortcut the drying process, place the baking sheet in the oven while it preheats to evaporate the remaining moisture from the chickpeas.

4. Once the chickpeas are dry, place them in a small mixing bowl with the olive oil and gently stir with a wooden spoon until coated. Season with salt, and gently mix. Return the chickpeas to the parchment paper–lined baking sheet and place it in oven to roast for about 40 minutes. Remove the baking sheet from the oven every 10 to 15 minutes and shake in a circular motion to

ensure even roasting. Remove from the oven when the chickpeas are a medium brown color and crispy when tasted. Set the tray on cooling rack for about 5 to 10 minutes.

5. Melt the chocolate chips in a small saucepan over low heat, stirring occasionally. Alternatively you can place the chocolate chips in a microwave-safe glass bowl and microwave on medium in 30-second increments, stirring after each increment. The chocolate should be completely melted and drip off the end of the spoon.

6. Line the baking sheet with a fresh sheet of parchment paper. Pour the melted chocolate in a small mixing bowl. Add the chickpeas while they are still warm. Stir with a wooden spoon until evenly coated and pour onto the baking sheet. Spread evenly with a spatula to the desired thickness of the bars. The bars cut best when about ¼- to ½-inch thick. Refrigerate 2 to 3 hours until the chocolate is solid. Remove from the refrigerator and cut with a sharp knife, or break into random pieces. Store in an airtight container at room temperature or refrigerate for up to 1 week.

Pure Piña Colada Bars

Makes 16 bars

Want to take a quick trip to a tropical paradise? These pineapple-coconut bars will have you feeling like your toes are in the sand. One of my favorite dessert bars, they're perfect sitting out on a platter while you're hanging out with friends and they'll bring a ray of sunshine to a rainy day.

Prep time: 20 minutes   **Cook time:** 35 minutes

3 tablespoons golden flaxseed meal

1/2 cup unsweetened plant-based milk (I use unsweetened cashew milk)

1 cup almond meal

1/2 cup coconut flour

1/3 cup coconut sugar

1/4 teaspoon finely ground sea salt

1/3 cup coconut oil, melted

2 teaspoons vanilla extract

1 3/4 cups chopped pineapple, drained, divided

1/2 cup Coconut Butter/Manna (page 21)

2 tablespoons coconut sugar

1/4 teaspoon vanilla extract

1/4 cup coconut flakes, for serving

1. Preheat the oven to 350°F. Grease an 8 x 8-inch baking pan with walnut, coconut, or grapeseed oil or line it with parchment paper and set aside.

2. In a small bowl, stir together the golden flaxseed meal and milk. Set aside.

3. In a medium bowl, combine the almond meal, coconut flour, 1/3 cup coconut sugar, and salt.

4. Add the coconut oil and 2 teaspoons vanilla to the flax egg mixture and whisk well. Add the wet ingredients to the dry ingredients and mix together with a spoon, fork, or pastry blender until the mixture is well combined and in crumbs like a graham cracker crust.

5. Place the chopped pineapple (reserving 1/4 cup), and coconut butter (stir before measuring if separated) in a food processor, and blend together. Add 2 tablespoons coconut sugar and vanilla. Mix well and set aside.

NOTES

- Canned pineapple may be substituted for fresh, but be sure to drain all of the juice.

- See my technique for measuring gluten-free flour (page 12) to ensure consistent measurements.

6. Press the crust firmly and evenly onto the bottom of the greased pan. Pour the topping over the crust and spread evenly. Sprinkle the remaining pineapple chunks and coconut flakes on top. Bake for about 35 minutes or until the center is slightly firm to the touch. Remove from the oven and allow to cool before cutting, about 1 hour. These bars are best served chilled. Store in an airtight container in the refrigerator for up to 1 week.

Tip: I like to top them with a dollop of Easy Coconut Whipped Cream (page 78) before serving.

Fresh Cranberry Crumb Bars

Makes 16 bars

SF

After first developing this recipe, I started storing bags of cranberries in my freezer once they became available during the holidays. Traditionally a late fall or early winter fruit, cranberries are impossible to find during the summer when I would routinely get requests to make these bars. With a fruity filling nestled between two layers of buttery crumbs, they are ideal for that sweet treat when the kids come home from school. I suggest making an extra batch for your holiday table.

Prep time: 30 minutes   **Cook time:** 30 minutes

1 cup almond meal

1 cup gluten-free oat flour

1/3 cup date or coconut sugar

1/4 teaspoon finely ground sea salt

3 tablespoons walnut oil or melted coconut oil

2 tablespoons unsweetened plant-based milk (I use cashew)

1 teaspoon vanilla extract

1 1/2 cups fresh cranberries (frozen can be substituted)

3/4 cup very ripe banana, approximately 1 large banana, fresh or frozen

1/2 cup coconut sugar

1 tablespoon vegan butter

1/4 to 1/2 teaspoon xanthan gum

1/4 teaspoon vanilla extract

1. Preheat the oven to 350°F. Grease an 8 x 8-inch pan with walnut, coconut, or grapeseed oil or line it with parchment paper.

2. In a medium or large bowl, combine the almond meal, gluten-free oat flour, date sugar, and salt and mix well with a spoon. In a small bowl, combine the walnut oil, plant-based milk, and 1 teaspoon vanilla, and mix thoroughly. Pour the wet ingredients into the dry ingredients and stir with a spoon until the mixture comes together in small pebble-size crumbs.

3. Reserve approximately 2/3 cup of dough for the crumble on top. Firmly press the remaining dough evenly into the pan. Set aside.

4. Wash and blot dry the fresh cranberries. Place the cranberries and banana in a food processor or a high-speed blender. Puree until smooth although the cranberry seeds may remain. Pour the cranberry-banana mixture into a small saucepan and warm over medium heat. When bubbles begin to appear, add the coconut sugar and butter. Blend with a whisk.

Continue whisking while cooking for an additional 2 to 3 minutes. Add the xanthan gum and whisk well. (I use ¼ teaspoon so the filling is not very thick, but you can adjust it to your liking.) Remove from the heat. Stir in the ¼ teaspoon vanilla.

5. Pour the cranberry mixture onto the crust in the pan and spread evenly with a spatula. Sprinkle the reserved crust crumbs on top and gently pat the dough pieces into the cranberry mixture. Place on the middle oven rack and bake for approximately 30 minutes.

6. When done, remove from the oven and place on a cooling rack for 45 minutes. It's advisable to refrigerate this before serving to allow the bars to firm up. After the bars have been refrigerated, they may be cut and served.

Fudgy Avocado Cookies

Makes 12 cookies (2-inch diameter) **OF** **SF**

All of the chewy chocolaty goodness of a brownie, wrapped in a light, crisp cookie shell. In my house, a batch typically does not make it to the next day. So, let's just go ahead and address the elephant in the room: No, you will not taste the avocado. However, be sure to use a *ripe* one, and preferably a Hass avocado, which will maximize the rich fat and creaminess while minimizing excess liquid.

Prep time: 10 minutes   **Cook time:** 9 minutes

1/2 ripe Hass avocado, peeled and cut into chunks

1/2 cup coconut sugar

2 rounded tablespoons unsweetened cocoa powder

2 teaspoons vanilla extract

1 teaspoon apple cider vinegar

1/2 teaspoon finely ground sea salt

1/2 teaspoon baking soda

1/2 cup almond meal

1/4 cup arrowroot

1/4 cup gluten-free oat flour

1/2 cup chopped vegan dark chocolate or vegan chocolate chips

> NOTE
> – See my technique for measuring gluten-free flour (page 12) to ensure consistent measurements.

1. Preheat the oven to 350°F and line a baking sheet with parchment paper.

2. Place the avocado in a food processor. Add the coconut sugar and blend until smooth, about 2 minutes. Be sure to scrape down the sides after 1 minute to assure that all avocado chunks have been blended. If you do not have a food processor, a medium mixing bowl and hand mixer may be used instead for all of the blending steps.

3. Add the cocoa powder, vanilla, vinegar, sea salt, and baking soda to the avocado and sugar mixture and blend until smooth, about 1 minute.

4. Add the almond meal, arrowroot, and gluten-free oat flour to the mixture and blend until smooth, about 1 minute.

5. Place the dough in a bowl, if using a food processor, and add in the chocolate chunks. Gently stir together with a spoon. Scoop tablespoon-size balls of dough onto the baking sheet. Flatten the cookie dough to approximately 2 inches in diameter and about ½ inch thick. If a more rustic cookie is desired, don't flatten, but bake the dough instead with small peaks. If a smooth cookie is desired, dip your fingertip in cold water and smooth the top of the cookies before baking. Bake for 9 minutes. Remove from the oven and allow the cookies to sit on the tray for 2 additional minutes. Then place the cookies on a cooling rack to continue cooling. The batch yield is about 12 cookies. Alternatively, 6 large 3-inch cookies can be made by increasing the baking time to 11 minutes.

Tip: *Selecting avocados:* When possible, I would encourage using Hass avocados to make these cookies and Creamy Avocado Fudge (page 230). They result in a richer and more substantial outcome. I do not advise using an avocado that has been refrigerated, as the earthy flavor becomes more pronounced and they are not as creamy.

Brookies

Servings: 16

SF

A Brookie? Yes. A chocolate chip cookie bottom with a fudgy brownie top. This recipe holds a very special place in my heart, being one of the first I developed for *Nutritionicity* and one that has been viewed millions of times. The recipe has two parts, and thus it may appear complicated, but it is not. These heavenly treats will be done in under an hour and bring out the kid in everyone!

Prep time: 25 minutes   **Cook time:** 15 minutes

CHOCOLATE CHIP COOKIE BOTTOM

1 cup almond meal

1 cup gluten-free oat flour

⅓ cup mini vegan chocolate chips

2 tablespoons coconut sugar

½ teaspoon baking soda

¼ teaspoon finely ground sea salt

3 tablespoons cashew butter or almond butter, melted

2 tablespoons coconut oil, melted

2 tablespoons coconut nectar, maple syrup, or brown rice syrup

1 tablespoon vanilla extract

(continued on the following page)

> **NOTE**
> – See my technique for measuring gluten-free flour (page 12) to ensure consistent measurements.

1. *Prepare the Chocolate Chip Cookie bottom:* Preheat the oven to 350°F. Grease an 8 x 8-inch pan with walnut, grapeseed, or avocado oil. In a medium bowl combine the almond meal, oat flour, mini vegan chocolate chips, coconut sugar, baking soda, and salt. Mix well with a wooden spoon.

2. In a small microwave-safe bowl melt the nut butter and coconut oil in the microwave for 45 seconds on medium-low. If you don't have a microwave you can use a small saucepan on the stove over a low heat.

3. Add the coconut nectar and vanilla to the melted cashew butter and coconut oil, and stir until blended.

4. Mix the wet ingredients into the dry ingredients with a wooden spoon. If you are having difficulty getting the ingredients to combine well, cut the ingredients

BROWNIE TOP

$\frac{1}{3}$ cup almond meal

$\frac{1}{3}$ cup gluten-free oat flour

$\frac{1}{3}$ cup unsweetened cocoa powder

$\frac{1}{4}$ teaspoon finely ground sea salt

3 tablespoons coconut oil

$\frac{1}{4}$ cup coconut nectar, maple syrup, or brown rice syrup

3 tablespoons unsweetened plant-based milk (I use cashew)

1 tablespoon vanilla extract

together like you would if making a pie crust, using a slicing motion with your spoon. Once combined it should be dry and crumbly like a graham cracker crust but stick together when pressed between your fingers. Firmly press the mixture onto the bottom of the greased pan.

5. *Prepare the brownie top:* In a medium bowl combine the almond meal, oat flour, cocoa powder, and salt. Mix well with a wooden spoon.

6. In a small microwave-safe bowl melt the coconut oil in the microwave for 30 seconds on medium-low or in a small saucepan on the stove over a low heat, and mix well with the dry ingredients using a wooden spoon. This will form a loose chocolate paste.

7. In a small bowl whisk together the coconut nectar, plant-based milk, and vanilla. Add to the chocolate paste and combine.

8. Pour the brownie mixture onto the chocolate chip cookie base and spread the batter over the cookie crust evenly.

9. Bake at 350°F for about 15 minutes. The brookies are done when a toothpick inserted in the center comes out clean. Remove from the oven and let cool for approximately 30 minutes. The Brookies can then be cut with a knife. For prolonged storage, place the bars in an airtight container and refrigerate for 5 to 7 days.

No-Bake Chocolate Chip Brownie Cheesecake

Servings: 12 slices

SF

Who doesn't love a challenge? Make a cheesecake without using any cream cheese? This recipe is proof there is no reason (or excuse) to force dairy products into your diet. You can experience the same dessert delights—taste, textures, and all—on a plant-based diet. This "cheesecake" has the same mouthwatering, smooth richness of a traditional recipe that leaves you longing for another slice. The tangy sweetness of the chocolate chip cake blends with the chocolaty goodness of the brownie crust. Simply divine!

Prep time: 30 minutes   **Cook time:** none

1 cup chopped dates

¼ cup golden raisins

1½ cups almond meal

½ cup unsweetened cocoa powder

1 tablespoon plus 2 teaspoons vanilla extract

½ teaspoon finely ground sea salt

1½ cups raw cashews, soaked

⅓ cup coconut oil, melted

⅓ cup coconut nectar (maple syrup may be substituted with a small flavor change)

¼ cup unsweetened cashew milk, or other mild-tasting plant-based milk

1 tablespoon plus 2 teaspoons lemon juice

1 teaspoon vanilla extract

(continued on the following page)

> **NOTES**
> – Soaking cashews is required prior to starting this recipe. See page 17 for quick-soak or overnight-soak instructions.
>
> – Total Time does not include time in the freezer.
>
>   **Pans:** I used a springform pan for easier removal, but a cake pan may be substituted. If a thicker cake is desired, a smaller pan can be used.
>
> – See my technique for measuring gluten-free flour (page 12) to ensure consistent measurements.

1. Lightly grease the bottom of an 8-inch cake pan or 9-inch springform pan with walnut or grapeseed oil and set aside. Add the dates and raisins to a small bowl and soak in hot water for about 5 minutes.

2. Drain the dates and raisins and place in a food processor. Blend until they are a pasty texture with

2 tablespoons coconut sugar

¼ teaspoon finely ground sea salt

½ cup vegan chocolate mini chips (more, about ⅓ cup, for drizzle, if desired)

some chunks, stopping to scrape the sides when necessary. Add the almond meal, cocoa powder, 1 tablespoon plus 2 teaspoons vanilla, and ½ teaspoon salt. Blend until a dough ball forms, stopping again to scrape the sides when necessary.

3. Remove the dough from the food processor. Press the dough into the bottom of the greased pan, flattening and spreading until the whole pan base is covered. Place the pan in the freezer while preparing the cheesecake filling.

4. Place the cashews in a food processor and blend until chunky. Add in the coconut oil, coconut nectar, and cashew milk and blend until smooth. Add the lemon juice, 1 teaspoon vanilla, coconut sugar, and ¼ teaspoon salt and blend until fully incorporated. Transfer the cake filling to a mixing bowl and stir in the chocolate chips. Remove the pan from the freezer and pour the cake filling on top of the crust. Spread evenly in the pan with a spatula. Place covered in the freezer for a minimum of 3 to 4 hours.

   If desired, prepare the drizzle. Melt the chocolate in a small microwave-safe bowl on medium-low or on the stovetop in a small saucepan over low heat and drizzle over the cake using a teaspoon. Return the cake to the freezer for 5 minutes to allow the drizzle to set.

   When ready to serve, remove the cake from the freezer and enjoy. If a softer texture is desired, allow to sit at room temperature for about 20 minutes.

Fudgy Chocolate Cake

Makes 12 slices

SF

There are a few things in life that almost everybody craves: pizza, burgers, and . . . chocolate cake. This luscious, creamy torte is easy to prepare and makes for an elegant presentation. So moist and delicious, this cake is wonderful on its own but would work well with any topping of your choosing. I suggest the Maple Caramel Drizzle that follows.

Prep time: 15 minutes   **Cook time**: 55 minutes

1 1/2 cups almond meal

1 1/2 cups gluten-free oat flour

1 cup coconut sugar

6 tablespoons unsweetened baker's cocoa

2 teaspoons baking soda

1 1/2 teaspoons salt

2/3 cup Medjool dates, pitted and broken into thirds

1/2 cup applesauce

3/4 cup walnut oil

2 tablespoons apple cider vinegar

1 tablespoon vanilla extract

1 1/2 cups cold water

MAPLE CARAMEL DRIZZLE (OPTIONAL)

1 tablespoon vegan butter spread

1 tablespoon cashew butter

1 teaspoon maple syrup

1 teaspoon vanilla

> **NOTE**
> – See my technique for measuring gluten-free flour (page 12) to ensure consistent measurements.

1. Preheat the oven to 375°F.

2. Combine the first six dry ingredients in a medium mixing bowl and mix well with a spoon, whisk, or mixer.

3. In a small bowl, soak the dates in very hot water for 5 minutes. This will help the dried fruit to break down more easily during pureeing. Drain the water before placing the dates in a food processor or high-speed blender. Add the applesauce and puree until smooth.

4. Make a well in the center of the dry ingredients. Add the date and applesauce puree and the walnut oil, vinegar, vanilla, and water.

5. Blend well with a mixer at medium speed until smooth, approximately 2 minutes.

6. Pour into an ungreased tube pan and bake for 50 to 55 minutes. When done, the cake should have a slightly crisp top, and a toothpick inserted in the center will only have a few crumbs or be clean.

7. Cool in the pan for 10 to 15 minutes, then remove the cake from the pan and place on a wire rack to complete cooling, approximately 1 hour.

8. If desired, make the Maple Caramel Drizzle. Melt the butter and cashew butter on the stovetop in a small saucepan over low heat. Add the maple syrup and vanilla to the melted butters and mix well with a spoon. Drizzle over the cake while still warm.

Creamy Avocado Fudge

Makes 25 one-inch cubes

I grew up appreciating and loving my mother's handcrafted fudge. While this recipe is dramatically different in ingredients from traditional fudge, the taste is identical. *Identical*. Being a fudge purist, I ensured this exquisite yet simple dessert is nothing short of a pure, chocolate delight. Plus with the addition of creamy avocado, it's indulgent but healthier too!

Prep time: 15 minutes   **Cook time:** 5 to 10 minutes

½ cup or about one half of a large ripe Hass avocado, pitted and peeled

1 ¼ cups vegan dark or semi-sweet chocolate chips

1 ½ teaspoons vanilla extract

½ cup coconut sugar

¼ cup unsweetened plant-based milk (mild tasting)

1 tablespoon vegan butter

1. Place the avocado in a food processor or high-speed blender and puree. Alternatively, the avocado can be mashed by hand but try to get it as smooth as possible. Place it in a small bowl and set aside.

2. In a medium mixing bowl, combine the chocolate chips and vanilla. Set aside.

3. In a small saucepan, whisk together the coconut sugar and plant-based milk. Add vegan butter and place over medium heat. Whisk continuously until at a rapid boil. Continue whisking over a rapid boil for 3 minutes. Add the avocado to the mixture, whisking in 1 tablespoon at a time until each is almost fully incorporated. Once the mixture is smooth, remove from the heat.

4. Pour the hot avocado mixture over the chocolate chips and vanilla and mix well with a spoon until completely combined and smooth. This may take a few minutes.

Tip: Add fun toppings like dried fruit and nuts in step 5 after spreading the fudge into the pan. My favorite additions include additional chocolate chips and walnuts.

5. Pour the fudge mixture into a 5 x 5-inch nonstick or greased pan. Avocado or grapeseed oil can be used to grease the pan. Spread the fudge evenly in the pan, smoothing the top with a spatula. Allow the fudge to sit at room temperature until cool. Cover with parchment paper and refrigerate for 8 hours or more until firm. Alternatively, the fudge may be placed in the freezer to accelerate the firming process.

Cocoa Almond Butter Cups

Servings: 24

I used to love peanut butter cups, but all of that refined sugar would eventually wreak havoc on me in any number of ways. When I first started contemplating ideas for plant-based and gluten-free recipes, I knew I needed to try to replicate those classic peanut butter cups. The result is this sweet pleasure—creamy almond butter wrapped in a chewy, sweet cocoa cake and crowned with a dollop of chocolate. They are a wonderful balance of sweet and salt. Not to mention, they are no-bake or raw, and party perfect!

Prep time: 20 minutes   **Cook time:** none

1 ½ cups almond meal, loosely packed

1 cup pitted Medjool dates, loosely packed

½ cup unsweetened cocoa powder

1 tablespoon plus 1 ½ teaspoons vanilla extract, divided

½ cup almond butter

1 tablespoon maple syrup

¼ teaspoon finely ground sea salt (small additional amount may be added, if desired)

½ cup vegan chocolate chips

> **NOTES**
> – Prep time does not include time for chilling.
> – See my technique for measuring gluten-free flour (page 12) to ensure consistent measurements.

1. In a food processor combine the almond meal and dates. Pause when necessary and scrape the sides. Blend together until mixed well and the dates are broken down. Add the cocoa powder and blend again until mixed. Add 1 tablespoon vanilla to the chocolate base and blend until the ingredients are uniformly mixed and begin to clump together.

2. Roll 1 tablespoon of the chocolate base into a ball in the palms of your hands and place it in one of the cups of a nonstick mini muffin tin. Press the ball down and spread to evenly line the bottom and sides of the muffin cup. I use the bottom of a round scoop to press the base into the tin. Continue filling the cups with the chocolate base. Place in the freezer while preparing the filling.

3. *To make the filling:* Wipe out the food processor container if any of the chocolate base remains. Then add the almond butter and maple syrup to the food processor and blend. Add 1½ teaspoons vanilla to the filling. Add the salt and blend until completely mixed, scraping the sides when necessary. Taste the filling and add additional salt or maple syrup if a saltier or sweeter filling is desired.

4. Remove the mini muffin tin from the freezer and place 1 teaspoon of filling on each chocolate base. Flatten with the back of a spoon until the top is even. Return to the freezer.

5. Melt the chocolate chips in a small microwave-safe bowl on medium-low or on the stovetop in a small saucepan over low heat. Remove the mini muffin tin from the freezer. Spoon 1 teaspoon of melted chocolate onto each cup. Freeze again until firm, about 20 minutes. These treats may be enjoyed chilled or at room temperature. They will keep for a week or more in an airtight container in the refrigerator.

Indulgent No-Bake Truffle Bites

Makes 25 1 1/2-inch bites

Years ago, if I saw one of those golden Godiva boxes sitting on a table, I would be drawn to it like a magnet. Today I still enjoy an occasional indulgence in a luscious confection, but these truffles let me do so without adding cream and refined sugar to my diet.

Prep time: 20 minutes   **Cook time:** none

1/2 cup packed pitted whole Medjool dates, about 9 large dates

1/2 cup raw cashews, soaked

1/2 cup almond meal

1/4 cup coconut flour

1/4 cup pecans

1/4 cup unsweetened plant-based milk

3 tablespoons coconut sugar

2 tablespoons golden flaxseed meal

2 tablespoons maple syrup

2 tablespoons almond or cashew butter

1 1/2 teaspoons vanilla extract, divided

1/8 teaspoon finely ground sea salt

1/2 cup coconut flakes

1 cup vegan chocolate chips, divided and melted

> **NOTES**
> - Soaking cashews is required prior to starting this recipe. See page 17 for quick-soak or overnight-soak instructions. I suggest using a quick-soak method for this recipe. The cashews can soak at the same time as the dates.
>
> - See my technique for measuring gluten-free flour (page 12) to ensure consistent measurements.

1. Line an 8 x 8-inch pan with parchment paper or grease with walnut or coconut oil.

2. Place the dates in a small bowl. Cover with very hot water and soak for about 30 minutes. Cashews can be soaked at the same time. Dates are ready when they are extremely soft. Rinse only the cashews, but drain both the cashews and the dates.

3. While the dates are soaking, place the almond meal, coconut flour, pecans, milk, coconut sugar, flaxseed meal, maple syrup, nut butter, 1/2 teaspoon vanilla, and salt in a food processor. Blend until completely combined. Transfer to an 8 x 8-inch pan and press evenly to cover the bottom. Set aside.

4. Place the cashews and dates, coconut flakes, and remaining 1 teaspoon vanilla in the food processor. Blend until smooth, about 3 to 5 minutes, scraping down the sides as needed.

5. Melt ½ cup chocolate chips in a small microwave-safe bowl on medium-low or on the stovetop in a small saucepan over low heat and spread evenly over the crust in the pan. Allow the chocolate to firm up. Place in the refrigerator for a couple of minutes, if necessary. Spread the cashew-date mixture evenly over the chocolate layer. Melt the remaining ½ cup of chocolate chips and spread on top. Refrigerate until all layers are firm, about 1 hour. Cut in 25 pieces and serve. Store the remaining bites in an airtight container in the refrigerator for 1 week or in the freezer for up to 2 months.

Luscious No-Bake Lemon Cheesecake

SF

Servings: 12

A dreamy and lush cheesecake with tangy, sweet notes of lemon rests upon a golden butter cookie crust. The individual serving sizes make it equally easy to plate for a dinner party or parse out for late-night treats on movie night.

Prep time: 25 minutes   **Cook time:** none

1 ½ cups raw cashews, soaked

3 large pitted Medjool dates

1 cup almond meal

1 cup gluten-free oat flour

½ teaspoon finely ground sea salt, divided

2 tablespoons refined coconut oil, melted

4 tablespoons coconut nectar (or substitute maple syrup, see Notes)

1 tablespoon vanilla extract, divided

¼ cup unsweetened plant-based milk (I use cashew)

¼ cup plus 1 tablespoon lemon juice

¾ teaspoon lemon zest

Tip: Coconut nectar and refined coconut oil do not add any coconut flavor to the dish.

NOTES

– Soaking cashews and dates is required prior to starting this recipe. See page 17 for quick-soak or overnight-soak instructions. Soaked raw almonds may be substituted for the cashews, but the skins will need to be removed after soaking and the overall flavor is not quite as creamy.

Substitutions: Maple syrup may be substituted for coconut nectar but will add some maple flavor.

– See my technique for measuring gluten-free flour (page 12) to ensure consistent measurements.

---

1. *Prepare the crust:* Five minutes prior to rinsing the cashews, place the dates in a separate small bowl with hot water and soak for the remaining time. Drain the dates but do not rinse.

2. Place the almond meal, oat flour, dates, and ¼ teaspoon salt in a food processor and mix together.

3. In a small bowl whisk or stir together the melted coconut oil, 2 tablespoons coconut nectar, and 2 teaspoons vanilla. Add to the wet ingredients in the food processor and mix together until blended and crumbly.

4. In a nonstick 12-count muffin tin or greased (with coconut oil) regular muffin tin, place 2 tablespoons of the crust mixture in each muffin cup and press down firmly and evenly to cover the bottom of the cup. Any remaining crumbs can be reserved for topping the cheesecakes. Freeze the crusts while making the filling.

5. *Prepare the filling:* Add the soaked cashews and 2 tablespoons coconut nectar, milk, lemon juice, 1 teaspoon vanilla, lemon zest, and ¼ teaspoon salt to the food processor. Blend until smooth, pausing occasionally to scrape the sides of the container, about 4 to 5 minutes.

6. Remove the muffin tin with the crusts from the freezer. Add 2½ tablespoons of filling to each cup and smooth evenly on the crust. Sprinkle the remaining crust crumbles on top of each cheesecake and place in the freezer. Freeze until firm, about 2 to 3 hours. Once firm, cheesecakes can be removed from the muffin tin by gently using a butter knife to remove the edges from the pan. If they do not easily come out of the pan, let them stand for 5 minutes and then remove. Store the cheesecakes in an airtight container in the freezer. They will keep for 3 to 4 weeks. Serve either directly from the freezer or allow to soften for a few minutes.

Healthier Chocolate Chip Cookies

Makes 18 two-inch cookies

Let's face it: A chocolate-chip cookie is not just a cookie—it's an experience. There is a reason it is universally considered the ultimate nibble. I refined this recipe batch after batch to achieve that optimal crispy shell and chewy inside, no milk and butter required. Best of all, these cookies are protein powerhouses, delivered from the Great Northern beans, oats, and sweet potatoes. A quick treat you can feel good about eating (and offering to your kids)!

Prep time: 15 minutes (not including baking the potato)   **Cook time:** 10 minutes per baking sheet

1 tablespoon golden flaxseed meal

3 tablespoons filtered water

1 cup Great Northern beans, rinsed and drained

1/2 cup gluten-free oats

1/2 cup white rice flour

2 teaspoons baking powder

1/2 teaspoon finely ground sea salt

1/2 teaspoon cinnamon

1/2 cup mashed cooked sweet potato

1/3 cup coconut sugar

2 tablespoons unsweetened plant-based milk

3 1/2 teaspoons vanilla extract

2 teaspoons apple cider vinegar

1/2 cup mini vegan chocolate chips, plus 1/4 cup (optional, to sprinkle on top of cookies)

> **NOTES**
> - *Advanced prep:* 1/2 cup of cooked mashed sweet potato will be necessary for this recipe. This can be baked a day ahead of time and refrigerated until use.
> - See my technique for measuring gluten-free flour (page 12) to ensure consistent measurements.

1. In a small bowl, whisk together the golden flaxseed meal and 3 tablespoons filtered water. Set aside.

2. Place the beans, oats, white rice flour, baking powder, salt, and cinnamon in a food processor and blend together.

3. Add the flax egg (flaxseed meal and water mixture), sweet potato, coconut sugar, milk, vanilla, and apple cider vinegar to the food processor and blend until smooth. Add the chocolate chips and pulse to mix into the dough. Some chocolate chips may break during the process. Alternatively, transfer the dough to a mixing bowl and stir the chips into the dough with a wooden spoon. Refrigerate the dough for 15 to 20 minutes.

4. Preheat the oven to 350°F. Line a baking sheet with parchment paper.

5. Portion 2 tablespoons of dough with two spoons and round into a ball. Place on the baking sheet and flatten the cookie to about ⅝ inch thick. Space the cookies at least 1 inch apart. If a smooth cookie is desired, dip your fingertip in cold water and smooth the top of the cookies before baking. If desired, sprinkle additional chocolate chips on the tops of the cookies and gently press. Bake for 8 to 10 minutes. More time will yield a crispy outside and soft center. Remove the baking sheet from the oven and place it on a cooling rack. After 2 minutes, remove the cookies from the baking sheet and place on the cooling rack to complete cooling. Store in an airtight container for 2 to 3 days or freeze for 1 month.

Tip: Great Northern beans are a very mild-tasting, creamy white bean. If substituting, it should be with a very mild-flavored white bean, such as cannellini.

Nutritional Data *for* Fruits

Raw, edible weight portion. Percent Daily Values (%DV) are based on a 2,000 calorie diet.

FRUITS Serving Size (gram weight/ounce weight)	Calories	Calories from Fat	Total Fat (g)	%DV	Sodium (mg)	%DV	Potassium (mg)	%DV	Total Carbohydrate (g)	%DV	Dietary Fiber (g)	%DV	Sugars (g)	Protein (g)	Vitamin A %DV	Vitamin C %DV	Calcium %DV	Iron %DV
Apple 1 large (242 g/8 oz)	130	0	0	0	0	0	260	7	34	11	5	20	25g	1g	2%	8%	2%	2%
Avocado California, 1/5 medium (30 g/1.1 oz)	50	35	4.5	7	0	0	140	4	3	1	1	4	0g	1g	0%	4%	0%	2%
Banana 1 medium (126 g/4.5 oz)	110	0	0	0	0	0	450	13	30	10	3	12	19g	1g	2%	15%	0%	2%
Cantaloupe 1/4 medium (134 g/4.8 oz)	50	0	0	0	20	1	240	7	12	4	1	4	11g	1g	120%	80%	2%	2%
Grapefruit 1/2 medium (154 g/5.5 oz)	60	0	0	0	0	0	160	5	15	5	2	8	11g	1g	35%	100%	4%	0%
Grapes 3/4 cup (126 g/4.5 oz)	90	0	0	0	15	1	240	7	23	8	1	4	20g	0g	0%	2%	2%	0%
Honeydew Melon 1/10 medium melon (134 g/4.8 oz)	50	0	0	0	30	1	210	6	12	4	1	4	11g	1g	2%	45%	2%	2%
Kiwifruit 2 medium (148 g/5.3 oz)	90	10	1	2	0	0	450	13	20	7	4	16	13g	1g	2%	240%	4%	2%
Lemon 1 medium (58 g/2.1 oz)	15	0	0	0	0	0	75	2	5	2	2	8	2g	0g	0%	40%	2%	0%
Lime 1 medium (67 g/2.4 oz)	20	0	0	0	0	0	75	2	7	2	2	8	0g	0g	0%	35%	0%	0%
Nectarine 1 medium (140 g/5.0 oz)	60	5	0.5	1	0	0	250	7	15	5	2	8	11g	1g	8%	15%	0%	2%
Orange 1 medium (154 g/5.5 oz)	80	0	0	0	0	0	250	7	19	6	3	12	14g	1g	2%	130%	6%	0%
Peach 1 medium (147 g/5.3 oz)	60	0	0.5	1	0	0	230	7	15	5	2	8	13g	1g	6%	15%	0%	2%
Pear 1 medium (166 g/5.9 oz)	100	0	0	0	0	0	190	5	26	9	6	24	16g	1g	0%	10%	2%	0%
Pineapple 2 slices, 3" diameter, 3/4" thick (112 g/4 oz)	50	0	0	0	10	0	120	3	13	4	1	4	10g	1g	2%	50%	2%	2%
Plums 2 medium (151 g/5.4 oz)	70	0	0	0	0	0	230	7	19	6	2	8	16g	1g	8%	10%	0%	2%
Strawberries 8 medium (147g/5.3 oz)	50	0	0	0	0	0	170	5	11	4	2	8	8g	1g	0%	160%	2%	2%
Sweet Cherries 21 cherries; 1 cup (140 g/5.0 oz)	100	0	0	0	0	0	350	10	26	9	1	4	16g	1g	2%	15%	2%	2%
Tangerine 1 medium (109 g/3.9 oz)	50	0	0	0	0	0	160	5	13	4	2	8	9g	1g	6%	45%	4%	0%
Watermelon 1/18 medium melon; 2 cups diced pieces (280 g/10.0 oz)	80	0	0	0	0	0	270	8	21	7	1	4	20g	1g	30%	25%	2%	4%

© U.S. Food and Drug Administration

Nutritional Data *for* Vegetables

Raw, edible weight portion. Percent Daily Values (%DV) are based on a 2,000 calorie diet.

VEGETABLES Serving Size (gram weight/ounce weight)	Calories	Calories from Fat	Total Fat g	Total Fat %DV	Sodium mg	Sodium %DV	Potassium mg	Potassium %DV	Total Carbohydrate g	Total Carbohydrate %DV	Dietary Fiber g	Dietary Fiber %DV	Sugars g	Protein g	Vitamin A %DV	Vitamin C %DV	Calcium %DV	Iron %DV
Asparagus 5 spears (93 g/3.3 oz)	20	0	0	0	0	0	230	7	4	1	2	8	2g	2g	10%	15%	2%	2%
Bell Pepper 1 medium (148 g/5.3 oz)	25	0	0	0	40	2	220	6	6	2	2	8	4g	1g	4%	190%	2%	4%
Broccoli 1 medium stalk (148 g/5.3 oz)	45	0	0.5	1	80	3	460	13	8	3	3	12	2g	4g	6%	220%	6%	6%
Carrot 1 carrot, 7" long, 1 1/4" diameter (78 g/2.8 oz)	30	0	0	0	60	3	250	7	7	2	2	8	5g	1g	110%	10%	2%	2%
Cauliflower 1/6 medium head (99 g/3.5 oz)	25	0	0	0	30	1	270	8	5	2	2	8	2g	2g	0%	100%	2%	2%
Celery 2 medium stalks (110 g/3.9 oz)	15	0	0	0	115	5	260	7	4	1	2	8	2g	0g	10%	15%	4%	2%
Cucumber 1/3 medium (99 g/3.5 oz)	10	0	0	0	0	0	140	4	2	1	1	4	1g	1g	4%	10%	2%	2%
Green (Snap) Beans 3/4 cup cut (83 g/3.0 oz)	20	0	0	0	0	0	200	6	5	2	3	12	2g	1g	4%	10%	4%	2%
Green Cabbage 1/12 medium head (84 g/3.0 oz)	25	0	0	0	20	1	190	5	5	2	2	8	3g	1g	0%	70%	4%	2%
Green Onion 1/4 cup chopped (25 g/0.9 oz)	10	0	0	0	10	0	70	2	2	1	1	4	1g	0g	2%	8%	2%	2%
Iceberg Lettuce 1/6 medium head (89 g/3.2 oz)	10	0	0	0	10	0	125	4	2	1	1	4	2g	1g	6%	6%	2%	2%
Leaf Lettuce 1 1/2 cups shredded (85 g/3.0 oz)	15	0	0	0	35	1	170	5	2	1	1	4	1g	1g	130%	6%	2%	4%
Mushrooms 5 medium (84 g/3.0 oz)	20	0	0	0	15	0	300	9	3	1	1	4	0g	3g	0%	2%	0%	2%
Onion 1 medium (148 g/5.3 oz)	45	0	0	0	5	0	190	5	11	4	3	12	9g	1g	0%	20%	4%	4%
Potato 1 medium (148 g/5.3 oz)	110	0	0	0	0	0	620	18	26	9	2	8	1g	3g	0%	45%	2%	6%
Radishes 7 radishes (85 g/3.0 oz)	10	0	0	0	55	2	190	5	3	1	1	4	2g	0g	0%	30%	2%	2%
Summer Squash 1/2 medium (98 g/3.5 oz)	20	0	0	0	0	0	260	7	4	1	2	8	2g	1g	6%	30%	2%	2%
Sweet Corn kernels from 1 medium ear (90 g/3.2 oz)	90	20	2.5	4	0	0	250	7	18	6	2	8	5g	4g	2%	10%	0%	2%
Sweet Potato 1 medium, 5" long, 2" diameter (130 g/4.6 oz)	100	0	0	0	70	3	440	13	23	8	4	16	7g	2g	120%	30%	4%	4%
Tomato 1 medium (148 g/5.3 oz)	25	0	0	0	20	1	340	10	5	2	1	4	3g	1g	20%	40%	2%	4%

© U.S. Food and Drug Administration

Sources

Barnard, Neal. *Dr. Neal Barnard's Program for Reversing Diabetes: The Scientifically Proven System for Reversing Diabetes Without Drugs.* New York: Rodale Books, Revised edition, 2018.

—. *The Cheese Trap.* New York: Grand Central Publishing, 2017.

Campbell, T. Colin and Campbell II, Thomas M. *The China Study.* Texas: BenBella Books, Inc., 2004.

Celiac Disease Foundation. https://celiac.org.

Davis, William. *Wheat Belly.* New York: Rodale, 2011.

Esselstyn Jr., Caldwell B. *Prevent and Reverse Heart Disease: The Revolutionary, Scientifically Proven, Nutrition-Based Cure.* New York: Penguin Group, 2008.

FoodData Central. https://fdc.nal.usda.gov/index.html.

Fratoni, Valentina and Maria Luisa Brandi. "B Vitamins, Homocysteine and Bone Health." Nutrients. April 7, 2015. https://www.ncbi.nlm.nih.gov/pmc/articles/PMC4425139/.

Fuhrman, Joel. "ANDI Food Scores: Rating the Nutrient Density of Foods." DrFuhrman.com. March 16, 2017. https://www.drfuhrman.com/get-started/eat-to-live-blog/128/andi-food-scores-rating-the-nutrient-density-of-foods.

Hyman, Mark, *10-Day Detox Diet.* New York: Little, Brown and Company, 2014.

Miao, M, B Jiang, S W Cui, T Zhang, and Z Jin. "Slowly digestible starch—a review." Critical Reviews in Food Science and Nutrition. 2015. https://www.ncbi.nlm.nih.gov/pubmed/24915311.

Naidoo, Uma. "Nutritional Strategies to Ease Anxiety." Harvard Health Publishing. April 13, 2016. https://www.health.harvard.edu/blog/nutritional-strategies-to-ease-anxiety-201604139441.

Venn, B J and Mann, J I. "Cereal grains, legumes and diabetes." European Journal of Clinical Nutrition. November 2004. https://www.ncbi.nlm.nih.gov/pubmed/15162131.

Vinoy, Sophie, Martine Laville, and Edith J M Feskens. "Slow-release carbohydrates: growing evidence on metabolic responses and public health interest." Food and Nutrition Research. 2016. https://www.ncbi.nlm.nih.gov/pmc/articles/PMC4933791/.

Wallace, Taylor C., Robert Murray, and Kathleen M. Zelman. "The Nutritional Value and Health Benefits of Chickpeas and Hummus." Nutrients. December 2016. https://www.ncbi.nlm.nih.gov/pmc/articles/PMC5188421/.

Acknowledgments

This book is in no way the work of one person. I am humbled by how many people have contributed their talent and effort to make it the completed book in your hands. There are so many to acknowledge.

To my readers who have been awesome cheerleaders and friends. Your enthusiasm for my recipes and touching stories inspired me to create this book. Thank you.

To my cherished friends and family members that gifted me unconditional support and unbridled passion. I appreciate you more than you will ever know.

My eternal gratitude to my agent, Pamela Harty, for taking on this project with such enthusiasm and shepherding me through the publication process skillfully. I couldn't have done it without your guidance and wisdom. Thanks also to Deidre Knight and all the fantastic folks at the Knight Agency.

To all the talented people I have had the honor of working with at Sterling Publishing. My editors: James Jayo—I will be grateful to you forever for making this dream a reality and sharing your vision with me. Nicole Fisher—I was so fortunate to be placed in your talented hands. Your keen eye and suggestions enhanced this book significantly. And the plant-based icing on the cake was that you were such a pleasure to work with! Jennifer Williams—your enthusiasm is contagious. Thank you for taking the reins without missing a beat. I am also filled with gratitude for my gifted project editor, Hannah Reich; copyeditor, Kimberly Broderick; and director of photography, Chris Bain. Thanks to Shannon Plunkett for such a fabulous design and layout and Elizabeth Lindy and David Ter-Avanesyan for cover design.

To Tim Coburn and James Cornwell for making author photo day so much fun.

Thanks to my colleague Richard Torregrossa, for taking me under his wing and patiently answering my many publishing questions.

A very special thanks to my mother, Beverly Smeby, for tirelessly acting as my chief recipe tester and believing that I can do anything. And my brother David Rudolph, for countless cross-continental brainstorming sessions and his genuine excitement and encouragement.

My wholehearted thanks to my husband, David, for sharing with me his gifts of writing and skillful editing when I struggled to get ideas out of my head and onto paper. I'm also grateful for all the other ways he helped me give this project legs—like sharing his dish-washing skills when he came home to a sink piled high, and tasting the fifteenth iteration of a recipe even when he wasn't hungry. Your help was indispensable.

And finally, to my son and daughter, Jacob and Megan, you were in the trenches with me every day, from the kitchen that was in a perpetual state of chaos to your questions that remained unanswered for hours at a time. My ad hoc photography assistant, Jacob, I couldn't have done the drizzle without you, and my super taster, Megan, no dish would be the same without your willingness to try it. I love you both more than I can ever put into words. Because of you, my heart is full.

About the Author

Jana Cristofano is a graduate of the University of Maryland at College Park and holds a certificate in Plant-Based Nutrition from Cornell University's T. Colin Campbell Center for Nutrition Studies. She is the writer and photographer of the popular plant-based/gluten-free food blog nutritionicity.com and a consultant and wellness advocate. Her recipes and knowledge have been featured in numerous web and print publications, including *Redbook*, *MSN*, *Country Living*, *Healthline*, *Closer*, *Huffpost*, and *Buzzfeed*.

Photo courtesy of David Cristofano

Index

Note: Page numbers in *italics* indicate photos separate from main recipe text.